ROYALTY IN CANADA;

EMBRACING

SKETCHES OF THE HOUSE OF ARGYLL,

THE RIGHT HONORABLE THE MARQUIS OF LORNE,
(Governor-General of Canada),

HER ROYAL HIGHNESS THE PRINCESS LOUISE

AND THE

MEMBERS OF THE NEW GOVERNMENT.

By CHARLES R. TUTTLE,

Author of " *The Comprehensive History of the Dominion of Canada,*"
" *Encyclopædia,*" *and other works.*

Janaway Publishing, Inc.
Santa Maria, California

Notice

In many older books, foxing (or discoloration) occurs and, in some instances, print lightens with wear and age. Reprinted books, such as this, often duplicate these flaws, notwithstanding efforts to reduce or eliminate them. The pages of this reprint have been digitally enhanced and, where possible, the flaws eliminated in order to provide clarity of content and a pleasant reading experience.

Copyright © 1878, Charles R. Tuttle

Originally published
Montreal, Canada
1878

Reprinted by:

Janaway Publishing, Inc.
732 Kelsey Ct.
Santa Maria, California 93454
(805) 925-1038
www.janawaygenealogy.com

2014

ISBN: 978-1-59641-323-8

Made in the United States of America

PREFACE.

It is desirable that the reader should know with what haste this little volume has been prepared. This, it is believed, will afford an ample apology for any defects which may appear.

On Tuesday afternoon of last week, the writer was requested to prepare a sketch of Her Royal Highness the PRINCESS LOUISE, and His Excellency the MARQUIS OF LORNE, the new Governor-General of the Dominion. On Wednesday morning, work was commenced in accordance therewith, and on Saturday evening of the same week the whole of the manuscript was completed. Mention is made of this, not as an evidence of rapid work, but as an excuse, on the part of the writer, for not furnishing a more perfect volume.

Notwithstanding the hurried manner in which it has been prepared, this little volume will present a very full sketch of the House of Campbell, of Her Royal Highness, the Princess Louise, and the Marquis of Lorne, and the members of the new Government of the Dominion, and will, perhaps, meet the want which it is intended to supply.

PREFACE.

The writer, however, regrets that as its publication upon a certain date was made imperative, no more time could be allowed him to perfect his work.

C. R. T.

MONTREAL, NOV. 9, 1878.

CONTENTS.

	PAGE
I.—INTRODUCTORY	17
II.—Story of the House of Argyll	33
III.—Sketch of the Right Honorable the Marquis of Lorne	75
IV.—Sketch of H. R. H. the Princess Louise	85
V.—Our new Governor-General	111
VI.—Canada—Political Situation	127
VII.—The Dominion Cabinet, 1878-9	153
VIII.—Parliamentary and Legislative Directory, etc., etc.	201

ILLUSTRATIONS.

PORTRAIT OF Her Majesty, Queen Victoria.
" " Her Royal Highness, the Princess Louise.
" " His Excellency, the Marquis of Lorne, Governor-General of Canada.
" " Gen. the Honorable Sir Patrick Macdougall.
" " Right Honorable Sir John A. Macdonald, K.C.B., Premier, and Minister of Interior.
" " Honorable Samuel L. Tilley, C.B., minister of Finance.
" " Honorable Charles Tupper, C.B., M.D., Minister of Public Works.
" " Honorable J. H. Pope, Minister of Agriculture.
" " Honorable John O'Connor, President of the Council.
" " Honorable James Macdonald, Minister of Justice.
" " Honorable L. F. R. Masson, Minister of Militia.
" " Honorable H. L. Langevin, Postmaster-General.
" " Honorable J. C. Pope, Minister of Marine and Fisheries.
" " Honorable Mackenzie Bowell, Minister of Customs.
" " Honorable J. C. Aikins, Secretary of State.
" " Honorable Alexander Campbell, Receiver-General.
" " Honorable L. F. G. Baby, Minister of Inland Revenue.

N. B.—These Portraits are neatly grouped together and printed on heavy plate paper, 22 x 28 inches in size, one copy of which is given with each copy of the book.

INTRODUCTORY.

A thrill of joy burst upon the Dominion with the announcement that a member of the Royal Family was coming to take up her abode in Canada. The nobleman himself,—The Right Honorable, the Marquis of Lorne, who was named to succeed the Earl of Dufferin, as our Governor-General,—was for the instant, overlooked in our enthusiastic rejoicing over the great compliment which Her Majesty paid to our loyalty in sending to us her beautiful and accomplished daughter, the Princess Louise. All hearts throbbed with a new interest. We felt that we were moving nearer to the throne of our Gracious Sovereign; that we were being rewarded, as a people, for our faithful obedience to the Crown: that we were rising to the full dignity of British citizenship; and our loyal hearts would fain have sent one long, broad, deep acclaim of WELCOME! across the ocean to greet the departure of Her Royal Highness.

In the midst of our joy at the coming of the princess there was but one feeling of regret, and we will be pardoned for referring to this at the very outset. It was consequent upon the departure from our

shores of their Excellencies the Earl and Countess of Dufferin. We can adopt the language of Thomas White, Esq., M.P., in reference to Lord Dufferin's administration and express the sentiment of the whole Canadian people: " It is only the simple
" truth to say that, of the nine statesmen who have
" represented Her Gracious Majesty in this country
" since the Union of 1841, Earl Dufferin succeeded
" best in winning the esteem and effection of the
" entire population. We do not make this statement
" for the purpose of detracting from the merits of
" his Lordship's illustrious predecessors. Every one
" of them had his characteristic gifts and graces, and
" they were all men of imperial distinction and re-
" nown. Some of them were quite equal to Lord
" Dufferin in those qualities which go to the making
" of statesmen. Almost all of them encountered
" during their career in Canada difficulties as trouble-
" some and dilemmas as puzzling as he did. But,
" in meeting the vexed questions of their times, we
" may assert, without exaggeration and without fear,
" that none of them displayed the same tact and put
" forth the same variety of power. He has the na-
" tural gift for ruling men, and he exercises it in a
" manner which renders his rule pleasing as well as
" firm. But the chief secret of the marked success
" which attended his whole administration was in
" the fact that he took a deep and a real interest in
" the country and the people. He always seemed to

INTRODUCTORY.

"identify himself with our progress. He always
"gave it to be understood, by word and act, that he
"had a share in our happiness, that our advance-
"ment in all that was best was to him a personal
"matter, in which his own well-being and pros-
"perity were concerned. His Government was as
"far as possible from being merely perfunctory. It
"was a pleasure to him to take part in anything in
"which the people were interested. This deep and
"constant interest in whatever touched, directly or
"indirectly, on our welfare, added to his many-sided
"culture and broad humanity, made him a model
"Governor. He sympathized with everything that
"was Canadian, and was himself as much Canadian
"as it was possible for him to be. In social life he
"was largely and generously hospitable, thus setting
"an example of the best taste. A scholar and au-
"thor, he took a lively interest in our educational
"progress and in our literary efforts. Even when
"about to receive an honorary degree from McGill
"University, he showed that he regarded the dis-
"tinction as something not merely formal by pre-
"paring himself for it. Indeed, his frequent pre-
"sence at our educational institutions, and his
"unaffected and hearty sympathy with which the
"success of our students, which he showed also in
"more substantial ways, have been the means of
"giving an impetus to the love of learning which,
"it is to be hoped, his memory will prevent be-

"coming weak. He was at home in all our manly
"sports, which he did more than any preceding Gov-
"ernor to encourage. He did much to strengthen
"our volunteer force by his ready co-operation in
"every movement that tended to its improvement.
"An artist, he was a cordial, as well as critical,
"patron of Canadian art. In fact, so numerous are
"the phases in which he manifested his desire that
"Canada should advance *pari passu* with the most
"civilized and growing of modern countries, that
"we cannot mention them all, and a simple account
"of the boons conferred by his potent and benefi-
"cent individuality on the Dominion, would resem-
"ble a panegyric or a picture of what a governor
"ought to be. Certainly such praise as this is ap-
"plicable to none of our previous viceroys, and to
"few who have ever occupied that high position
"anywhere."

The great regard entertained by all Canadians for their Excellencies the Earl and Countess of Dufferin must be a sufficient apology for this digression. The regret felt at their departure, however, was more than counterbalanced by the joy consequent upon the appointment of their successors. It has long been a cherished hope that one of Her Majesty's sons or daughters should be sent to Canada, and now that this hope has been realized, Canadian loyalty will experience new growth. Beyond this, we may expect that, with a nobleman of well known literary tastes and ability, and a Princess whose artistic skill is universally acknowledged, filling the most important station in the Dominion, a spirit of culture will be developed and the circle of the educated and refined, elevated and expanded.

From a social point of view, the presence of the Princess cannot fail to produce the very best results. In what we call fashionable circles, just now, there is a decided tremor of agitation as to how accessible Rideau Hall will be to society during her residence here. We all know that society worshipped Lord and Lady Dufferin, and it may be that their success in this respect will make it difficult for their successors. In their time there were many dinners, balls, at-homes, theatricals, concerts and skating parties, which were so generously managed as to gather in society in a most liberal extent. Indeed so wide was the hospitality of Rideau Hall, that some of the more exclusive were, on more than one occasion, heard to complain that the circle surrounding it was rather two elastic. These are now congratulating themselves upon an expected change, while, on the other hand, those who constituted the real heart and life of society in its broadest days, are in doubt as to whether Her Royal Highness will encourage or subdue them. It is believed by some, and not without reason, that the appointment of the Marquis is but the precursor of a genuine Royal Governor-General, and that, in due course he will be succeeded by the Duke of Edinburgh, and that he will be made a permanent viceroy. Certainly such a forecast augurs well for the social position of Canada. If realized, it would create a most delightful social life; noble families would probably be induced to come to Canada; while wealthy and aristocratic persons throughout the Dominion would move to Ottawa; and there would undoubtedly be an influx, at certain seasons, of the richest families from the large American cities.

There are those who rejoice at the prospect of all this, while on the other hand, one will not unfrequently meet with those who regret it on these grounds: they fear that the splendor and expense of a household befitting the rank of royalty will bring about a taste for extravagant display on the part of the people of Canada, which they have not the means to gratify. But these things will regulate themselves. Whether we shall have another member of the Royal Family to succeed the Princess, will very much depend upon the results of this experiment. Those who take alarm at the prospect of extravagence have no grounds for serious fears. The Marquis is a nobleman of considerable wealth, but his training and the examples set for him by a long line of illustrious ancestors, are such as to warrant the belief that his administration will not be characterized by needless expenditure, and it must be well known to all that the salary of the Governor-General

INTRODUCTORY.

is not sufficient to defray even the necessary expenses of the post. The Princess, on the other hand, received but £30,000 as her dower, and the scanty allowance of £6,000 per annum, granted by parliament. These facts, together with the principles of economy which have always been shown by Her Majesty, the Queen, seem to warrant, beyond any doubt, that the conduct of Her Royal Highness, while in Canada, will be in keeping with her responsibilities to this country.

But after all, we must not expect that the Princess will fill the same place in the social world that Lady Dufferin occupied; nor that she will be, in any large degree, accessible by those who most display themselves in society. This would not be suitable to her rank. It would be simply impossible. While in this country she will, in a higher sense than is possible to His Excellency the Governor-General, represent Her Gracious Majesty; and we have no right to expect any conduct at her hands that would be unbecoming the Sovereign herself. The Princess, at the English Court, and the Princess at Rideau Hall must, in the nature of things, be very different; and this difference will not bring her nearer to the people, but rather elevate her still higher above them. At the former station she can be, at most, but a Princess; at the latter she will be all that and far more. She will be our Queen! and we should prepare ourselves to receive her as we should Her Majesty the Queen!

But these views of the great dignity which must necessarily surround the person of the Princess, while in Canada, should produce no fears in the fashionable circle. There will be no restraint upon society, no subducing of Canadian aristocracy. Nothing of the kind. On the contrary, the presence of the Princess at Ottawa will impart a new life, a new brilliancy to the social circle. She will be the centre of a grand social sentiment, the rallying point for a rising aristocracy; and yet the court of Her Royal Highness will not be accessible, except to those of special rank and position. We must reconcile ourselves to this change. We must learn to discriminate between rank and Royalty. The latter can be maintained in proper regard only by keeping its imperial head above the nobility. We have had a Countess, but never before a Princess, at Rideau Hall. We have had nobility, but never before Royalty, at our vice-regal Court.

The presence of the Princess in Canada will have more than a social significance; it will have great political influence. It will carry us through that transition state where our destinies seem to be balancing between Imperialism and Republicanism. It will arrest our drifting into the Republic of the United States. This statement should not be thought significant of existing disloyalty among the Canadian

INTRODUCTORY. 25

people. Strictly speaking there is not a trace of such in the whole Dominion. But it would be strange, indeed, if after such a lengthy period of commercial union as we have had with the United States, we should not find ourselves tending Republicward. It is a common political doctrine in the United States that we are ultimately to join that country, and increase the number of Republican United States in America; and the governmental policy of our neighbors has always kept this end in view. So long has this been the case that leading American journals have come to speak of our supposed Republican destiny as a matter of course. In proof of this we may quote from the New York *Herald*, of September 28 last, when that journal upon the occasion of the triumph of the Liberal Conservative party of this country at the polls, remarked, that, " even as simple
" spectators so surprising a political change in a
" neighboring people would be a curious object of
" attention. The politics of Canada touch us more
" nearly than the politics of Germany or Italy or
" Russia or Turkey, to which we are not indifferent,
" although they have but a remote bearing upon our
" own prosperity. Canada is our neighbor and some-
" thing more. She naturally belongs to our political
" system; her destiny, either near or remote, will
" make her a valued member of our great family of
" free States. We must always take a lively interest
" in her affairs and watch with keen attention the

"political winds which drive her off her course and
"impede or postpone the fulfilment of her destiny."

It is somewhat interesting to observe the assurance of this newspaper. It may be a little consoling to learn that we are to be a "valued member" of a "great family of free states," but by far the greater portion of the Canadian people will rejoice most in the recent "political winds which have driven us off our [*Yankee*] course." These winds have, indeed, as the *Herald* has recently observed, been two-fold. First there comes the national policy or high tariff wind. This gale, if it shall continue to blow, will in the estimation of our neighbors,—and they are certainly correct for once,—make sad havoc with our "destiny." The other wind, (and "it never rains but it pours") is the wind of Royalty,—the appointment of the Marquis of Lorne and the Princess Louise to preside at Rideau Hall. It is not a little gratifying to us, and disheartening to our ambitious neighbors, that steps have been taken simultaneous by the Imperial Government and Canadian people to save the Dominion from the designs of Republican Statesmen. The movement has produced the greatest fears among the Americans, that they may after all, be mistaken about the destiny of Canada. Irritated at the signs of the times the New York *Herald* applies itself seriously to argument, perhaps, in the hope of persuading us to join the Republic. It says: "The population of the seven provinces

INTRODUCTORY.

"which constitutes the Dominion of Canada is con-
"siderably less than that of our six New England
"States, and the two regions are not dissimilar in
"soil, climate and natural productions. It will be
"conceded by every intelligent man in Canada, as
"readily as by every intelligent man in the United
"States, that it would be a fatal and prostrating blow
"to New England to separate her from the Union
"in the same manner that Canada is separated and
"deprive her of free access to our markets. If the
"New England States were put out of the American
"Union, if they could not introduce their manufac-
"tures for sale in our markets without the payment
"of heavy duties, their population would dwindle
"in a few years to less than half its present amount.
"If Canada were taken into the Union and New
"England excluded the two would exchange not
"merely their political relations, but their in-
"dustries and prosperity. There is nothing which
"could happen to Canada which would so promote
"its industrial development, so enhance the value
"of every acre of its property, or impart such an
"impetus to the growth of its population, as to give
"it the same free access to the whole vast extent of
"the American market that is enjoyed by our New
"England States. This is so obvious that a mere
"statement is equivalent to an argument; so ob-
"vious on its face that the most elaborate arguments
"could add nothing to the force of conviction. It is

" so self-evident that all the great interests of New
" England would be ruined by severance from the
" Union and isolation, like that suffered by Canada,
" that no sane mind would think of disputing it ;
" and how can anything be good for our neighbors
" which would be fraught with such mischief to a
" corresponding section of our own country ? "

Here we have the leading journal of the United
States declaring to us that *there is nothing which
could happen to Canada, which would so promote its
industrial development, so enhance the value of every
acre of its property, or impart such an impetus to the
growth of its population as to give it the same free
access to the whole vast extent of the American market
that is enjoyed by the New England States.* This statement is not to be wondered at, and the Americans
are best qualified to appreciate whatever of truth
there may be in it, for they have themselves had the
full benefit of whatever market advantages Canada
could furnish, for many years, without suffering the
inconvenience of giving us any return. The question for Canadian statesmanship to solve is this : at
what price are these American market advantages to
be purchased ? If at the cost of our loyalty to the
Crown and Kingdom of Great Britain, as the American political policy indicates, then we will refuse to
make the purchase, and endeavor to expand and
strengthen on our own markets by protecting them
from the ravages of Yankee competition ; by protect-

ing our own industries, and in that manner stopping the flow of our population to a foreign country. And we are to be congratulated that in this work which we have already begun we shall have the encouraging presence of a member of the Royal Family of our Gracious Queen.

The Americans have caught the spirit of the political reaction in Canada, and, with their usual keen observation, see plainly that we are in earnest. Hence, always interested in our welfare, they proffer advice which, we presume will not be highly appreciated : "It would be wiser in the interest of pro-
" tection itself to 'make haste slowly.' A moderate
" enhancement of duties at the outset would be
" safer, since he (Sir John A. Macdonald) needs to
" provide against a reaction. If he should carry a
" high tariff through Parliament, causing a large
" amount of capital to be embarked in new manu-
" facturing establishments, and then should be thrown
" out of power before the new establishments got
" into successful operation, the owners of the misdi-
" rected capital would denounce him for their ruin.
" If he is the wise and cautious statesman that we
" suppose him to be, he will begin with moderate
" protective duties and wait to see whether the
" policy on which his party has been elevated to
" power expresses the deliberate and stable convic-
" tions of the Canadian people. If he is really an
" astute and far sighted statesman, the use he will

" make of his strong protectionist majority will be
" to employ it as an instrument for securing trade
" advantages in a new reciprocity treaty with the
" United States."

In the last sentence above we already have signs of good results for the high tariff policy. This journal at least throws out the desire to renew reciprocity,—a thing which the States have long refused to do,—rather than be excluded from Canadian markets altogether. But we find ourselves drifting into questions which have unfortunately become too partisan.

Lastly, the presence of the Princess Louise in Canada, as the Consort of the Governor-General, will raise the Dominion higher in the estimation of all nations. It will identify us with the Mother Country, and bring us into greater importance as a part of the United Kingdom.

But while our noble Princess will receive the best homage of every Canadian heart, the young Lord of Lorne will also have the enthusiastic admiration of the whole population. We shall discriminate between Rank and Royalty only in so far as becomes British subjects. The Marquis is our Governor-General, and he will be sure to receive all the more respect, as such, because accompanied by the Princess. Some one has written a quaint welcome for them both, which recently appeared in the Montreal *Daily*

Witness. It is worthy to be accorded a place in the *Lorne literature* of the day :

A WELCOME.

Gather, oh gather! gather, oh gather!
    On with the philabeg every man,
Up with the bonnet and badge of your father,
    Belt on the plaid of the great Campbell clan
From the fair heather-clad hills of that Island,
    In whose straths and glens your fathers were born,
They come—so gather, ye hearts that are Highland,
    Welcome the Lord and the Lady of Lorne!
        Gather, oh gather, &c.

From ocean to ocean welcome is ringing,
    Fair Indian summer with blush and with smile,
O'er the forest her right royal vesture is flinging,
    To welcome the bride of the heir of Argyll.
The Princess of Lorne, we rise to receive her
    First Royal lady our country has seen,
To the wild land of the maple and beaver
    We welcome the Princess, thou child of our Queen.
        Gather, oh gather, &c.

We had regret which we sought not to smother,—
    Kind Earl and dear Countess were called to depart;
Thoughtfully, kindly, the fair Queen our mother,
    Sends the son of her choice, the child of her heart.
There is a stir, a bustle, a humming,
    Tartans are waving, plumes floating free,
Trumpet and drum sound "The Campbells are coming,"—
    We are all Campbells in welcoming thee.
        Gather, oh gather, &c.

Son of Argyll, so near to the sceptre,
    Princess Louise, fair child of a throne,
Welcome to stand for our Queen in this empire,
    Rule us, and love us, and make thine own.
Blow up, oh wild pibroch that welcomes no other!
    Shout million-voiced welcome, wave banners the while!
She is worthy, fair child of so Royal a mother,
    He is worthy the name and fame of Argyll,
            Gather, oh gather, &c.

STORY OF THE HOUSE OF ARGYLL.

THE Campbells constitute the most numerous clan in Scotland. The first of the house mentioned in authentic history is Gillespie Campbell, grandson of another Gillespie. His name is recorded in the Statutes of Alexander I. of the Thirteenth Century; but there can be no doubt that it was left to his great-grandson, styled Sir Colin Campbell of Lochow, to establish the family greatness. From Sir Colin the race of Campbell chieftains received the title of MAC-COLIN-MORE (Macallummore), or sons of Colin the Great. In documents dated as far back as 1293, he is styled "Dominus Campbell Miles," which shows that the family name was the same as it is now. His very active career was marked chiefly by the large accessions which he made to the estate of his house by those bitter disputes with the Macdougals of Lorne, which resulted ultimately in the overthrow of the latter tribe, and by the sacrifice of his own life in a battle with the Lord of Lorne, in which the Campbells, infatuated with victory, pursued their gallant foes too far, and witnessed the fall of their brave chieftain at a place called the String of Cowall, where an obelisk was erected over his grave.

But we must go back beyond Sir Colin Campbell and the annals of the Thirteenth Century to find the origin of the Campbell clan, and after we have done this we shall be compelled to regard the results of our investigation somewhat uncertain. The clan has without doubt absorbed, and holds to this day, many families which do not belong to it by blood or actual descent. Smaller clans, awed or won into submission by the great power possessed by the heads of the house, attached themselves to it, and threw off their distinctive titles and names; and, while this remark applies for the most part to the commonalty, it may be held to refer in a considerable degree to the gentry also.

It is a matter of astonishment that the origin of the Campbells and that of their name has not yet been fully settled. The general view of most genealogists is that they come from a Norman named *De Campo-Bello*. In relation to this point a recent English author observes that, "Whe-
"ther the first Campbells were or were not Normans may
"be disputed, but there seems little reason to doubt that the
"name was compounded in one of the ways mentioned. It
"is not unlikely that some distinguished feat in war was
"the honourable source of the designation. Some con-
"queror of a battlefield may actually have left it to his
"posterity. It may have been given, however, by a Scot-
"tish as well as a Norman monarch. The evidence of
"Norman descent, it must on the whole be admitted, is
"incomplete, but the advocates of a Gaelic origin have no
"better testimony to present on their side. The name does
"not occur in the older authentic Norman lists. It is
"found in Ragman Roll, nevertheless, and it then appears
"as CAMBEL, a word which no author, we believe, has ever
"attempted to trace to the Gaelic language, and which is
"most unlike the ordinary clan denominations. Some
"authors take it to be the same name with Beauchamp;
"and certainly the conjecture is no very improbable one,
"Campus-Bellus being, in one sense, that name Latinized.

"The advocates of this view say that a Gaelic chief wedded a Beauchamp heiress, and took her family designation. But, whatever the founders of the house might be by birth, the Campbells became thoroughly Gaelicized, beyond all question, in the progress of time; and, with their offspring and followers, they have long formed one of the greatest and most illustrious of the septs of the Highlands."

The generally accredited account of the origin of the Campbells is that the first of the name married the heiress of O'Duin (spelled O'Dwin, O'Duibne, and other ways), and in this way became Lord of Lochow, in the district of Argyll. And here we are reminded that O'Duin points us to an Irish origin. It is supposed that the tribe named here was among those which, at a very early period, emigrated from Ireland to the West Highlands of Scotland. Some very good authorities tell us that these O'Duins were Lords of Lochow. The authority last quoted says the personage who founded the O'Duin sept, or at least raised it to importance, was named Diarmid, and hence arose the title of SIOL DIARMID (Race of Diarmid), which the Gael have bestowed ever since on the Campbells. Diarmid was followed by a long line of powerful descendants, until, at length, the succession terminated in an heiress, EVA, whose hand was bestowed on GILLESPIE CAMPBELL, a gentleman commonly styled of Anglo-Norman lineage. With his bride he obtained the lordship of Lochow; and unquestionably the territory remains to this day the centre of the Campbell possessions. Such is the tale ordinarily told, at all events; and we must candidly say that no better one, at least, appears to us to have been yet put in its place.

Sir Niel Campbell, son of Sir Colin, succeeded him, and

became one of the main supporters of King Robert Bruce. This was a lucky stroke of policy for the Campbells. Sir Niel soon raised himself so high in the king's estimation as to receive the hand of his sister, Lady Mary, in marriage. This matrimonial alliance, like that which has occurred in our own time, between the House of Argyll and the reigning house of Great Britain, marked the commencement of a new era in the fame of the Campbells. From that hour their advancement, political and social, was rapid and substantial. Nor was this advancement from very mean beginnings. In 1821, their influence with Alexander II. had been quite sufficient to obtain the hereditary Sheriffdom of Argyll. But their intermarriage with the Bruces gave fortune and fame. Sir Niel, for his services in the cause of the King, was remunerated with lands, extending nearly into the heart of Athol. He was one of the Barons composing the parliament of Ayr in 1315, after having treated with the English at York, in 1314, for the establishment of peace.

Sir Niel was succeeded by his son Sir Colin Campbell, who, like his father, distinguished himself in the Bruce wars. A story is told of him, that on one occasion he incurred the wrath of his royal uncle. " The Scottish army
" was passing through a wood, in February, 1317, and King
" Robert issued strict orders that no man should leave the
" ranks. Galled by the shot of two English bowmen, how-
" ever, the young Campbell started forth at full speed to
" take vengeance upon them personally. The King followed
" and struck his nephew so violently with a truncheon that
" he was nearly unhorsed, crying at the same time, ' Return!
" your disobedience might have brought us all into jeopardy.'
" In sooth, both as a general and a knight, Robert the Bruce
" was well worthy, in old Barbour's words, to be ' the king
" of a great royalty.' "

The head of the family of Campbells was summoned to Parliament in the year 1445, as a peer of the realm. It is not certain but that the creation of the title may have taken place previously, but in the case of the Campbells, as also of nearly all the old barons of Scotland, the summons of 1445 constitutes the first authenticated proof of the parliamentary title. In this instance " LORD CAMPBELL " was the style adopted and Sir Duncan Campbell was the first to wear the title. But if care was taken during the regency under the minority of James II. to define the position and titles of noblemen, that monarch, on assuming the crown, exercised a still greater solicitude in this respect. When he became of age, he raised Colin, the grandson and heir of Duncan, to the dignity of EARL OF ARGYLL. This was in 1457.

It was at this period that the Lorne estates came into the possession of the Campbells, which happened in this way. Colin Campbell, Earl of Argyll, married the co-heiress of the Stewarts of Lorne, the immediate successors of the Macdougalls. Thus it was, that while the Stewarts were the immediate successors of the purely Gaelic occupants of these lands, it was destined that the Campbells should ultimately supplant them. " There can be no doubt," says a reliable author, " about these circumstances. Charters under the Great Seal are still extant, proving that the heir-male of the house of Stewart of Lorne made such concessions as gave to his neice and her husband nearly the entire barony which has been the property of the Campbells ever since. A natural son of the house of Stewart, however, contrived to retain some of the family possessions, founding the Appin and other branches of that name.

But as we have already observed, that the possessions of the Macdougalls came into the hands of the Campbells, through the Stewarts, their immediate successors, we must turn aside for a few moments to make some observations concerning that ancient and illustrious clan; and in this instance we shall make some extracts from John Hogg, Esq., a somewhat noted author :—

It seems very evident that they formed one of the primitive branches of the roving or stranger tribes of visitants to Scotland of the Irish or at least Celtic race. Their name puts the fact almost beyond doubt. It also distinguishes them clearly from the Norseman of the Western Isles, who were always styled *Fion-Galls*, that is, fair strangers (Rovers or Pirates). The yellow-haired Kempions of Scandinavia, in all their own early annals relating to Scotland, are not to be mistaken for the Celtic *Dhu-Galls*, or Black Strangers. The common account of the origin of the Macdougalls is, that they sprung from a son or grandson of Somerled, of the name of Dougal. But, though a single chieftain of that appellation may have flourished in the primitive periods of Gaelic story, it appears most probable, from many circumstances, that the clan derived their name from their descent and character generally. They were Dhu-Galls, black strangers. They are thus to be found giving a permanent title to GALLOWAY, for example. where many of their descendants hold lands to this day.

The Dhu-Galls or Dougals were so powerful as to maintain a long contest with Robert Bruce for supremacy in Scotland ; and, indeed, his hardest struggle, during his entire struggling life, was with the Argyllshire or Lorne Macdougals. In truth, it was but natural that they should have had an antipathy to him, as the representative of a different race and different interests. He was of English or Norman blood, a member of one of those families brought into Scotland by the policy of the Lowland monarchs, in order to sustain them against the hostile and purely Celtic population of the north and north-west Highlands. Historians have been too apt to view the contests in the early Bruce and Stewart times as contests betwixt individual *chiefs* ; whereas, in reality, they were the struggles of two distinct and opposing *races*. The Dhu-Galls, the Gael of Argyllshire, tried long to maintain the battle with the Norman Bruces. They were unsuccessful; though, when driven to plant their power in the more northerly and inaccessible isles of the west, the very same race (under the Lords of the Isles) kept up the engagement afterwards for centuries with the Stewart kings. The battle was that of Gael against Norman and Saxon—the Celtic against the Gothic race. It matters not whether the Celt was primitively from Ireland or from Gaul ; or whether the Lowlander was the offspring of Saxon, Dane, or Norman. The Celtic and Gothic races, under whatever denominations they might be ranked, were the two great parties that struggled against each other for supremacy in the early days of Scottish history. In spite of their brilliant though irregular valour, and a fine idealism of intellect, the Celts were overborne. The fact cannot be gainsayed. The whole annals of the overthrow of the Roman empire tell the same tale. Being placed on the mainland from the first, seemingly, and close to the Lowland power, the particular tribe of the Dhu-Galls which took the permanent name of Macdougals fell before the southron encroachments, at a period long preceding the similar fall of the Macdonalds of the Isles. The Macdougals had their chief seat in Lorne, or the centre of the continent of Argyllshire, betwixt Loch Awe and the seas of the west. The son or grandson of Somerled, who is said to have specially founded the Macdougal clan, lived in the twelfth century. In the thirteenth, however, they were numerous and strong enough to oppose Bruce, and it is therefore out of the question to suppose that the descendant of Somerled could do more than consolidate or collect an already existing tribe, even if it is to be admitted as taking from him its name. His grandson, or immediate successor, Alexander, is said to have been the chief who led the Macdougals in the wars against the Bruces. After King Robert Bruce was crowned at Scone, in 1306, the forces of Edward I. of England attacked and overthrew him, compelling him to fly to the west of Scotland, with the view of seeking refuge in Ireland, which country had then a common interest in resisting the English. But Alexander Macdougal of Lorne encountered him at a place called Dalree, on the borders of Argyllshire, and a fierce combat ensued between the parties. Bruce is described by Barbour as performing a truly heroic part on the occasion, though worsted and compelled to retreat. He rescued the flying, and checked so the pursuers—

> 'That none durst out of battle chase,
> For always at their hand he was.
> So well defended he his men,
> That whosoe'er had seen him then
> Prove so deserving of vassalage,
> And turn so often the visage,
> He should say he ought well to be
> The King of a Great Royalty.'

But Bruce fought in vain, and indeed escaped with life almost miraculously in the end. Three of the clansmen of Lorne, who seem to have been personal attendants or *henchmen* of the chief of the Macdougals, resolved that they would either slay the sovereign or die. They followed the retreating party, accordingly, and when Robert entered a narrow pass, riding behind his people, in what certainly was the post of danger for the moment, the three *Macindrossers* (otherwise called Macanorsoirs, the Mackeoghs, but sons of the *Door-ward*, or door-keeper to the Macdougal chieftain) threw themselves upon the monarch at once. One of them was instantly rewarded with such a blow of the royal battle-axe that " arm and shoulder flew him frae." The second had grasped the stirrup, and Robert fixed and held him there by pressing down his foot, so that the captive was dragged along the ground as if chained to the horse. In the meantime, the third assailant had sprung from the hillside to the back of the horse, and sat behind the king. The latter turned half-round and forced the Macindrosser forward to the front of the saddle, where he clave the head to the harns. The second assailant was still hanging by the stirrup, and Robert now struck at him vigorously, and slew him at the first blow. The arm of a single man has seldom done such a feat as that here narrated, and the probable truth of which is confirmed by the death of the young Bohun at Bannockburn, and other similar actions of Bruce.

The Macdougals were victors in the general combat which thus terminated. But Alexander of Lorne had taken up the losing side. The Lowland power was daily advancing in strength, and the Dhu-Galls sank before its progress. It was about the period mentioned, if not in the actual battle described, that the famous Brooch of Lorne came into the family of the Macdougals. It is said to have been a personal ornament of Robert Bruce; and, when the cloak of the retreating monarch

was grasped by one or other of his assailants, the brooch by which it
was fastened fell into the hands of his pursuers. If Barbour tells the
tale aright (and as it has been here recorded), the immediate assailants
paid with their lives for their audacity; but the cloak and brooch
were found by others of the enemy, and kept long thereafter, as a monument of victory, by the chiefs of the house of Macdougal. General
Stewart of Garth tells us that the brooch was lost or destroyed when
Dunolly Castle was burned down in the seventeenth century. However, the Brooch of Lorne has reappeared within these latter years, and
has even been exhibited publicly in the capital of Scotland. It is described as being of silver, not of gold, as said by Scott in the Lord of
the Isles. His words are—

> Whence the Brooch of burning gold,
> That clasps the chieftain's mantle fold,
> Wrought and clasped with rare device.
> Studded fair with gems of price,
> On the varied tartan beaming,
> As, through night's pale rainbow gleaming,
> Fainter now, now seen afar,
> Fitful shines the morning star.

But the Brooch of Lorne, as observed, proves not to be of gold, but of
silver, and we are inclined strongly to look upon the fact as a proof of
the authenticity of the article discovered of late years, and honoured
with the title of the Brooch of Robert Bruce, lost by him in contest
with the followers of the family of Lorne. A manufacturer of such
articles would scarcely have gone counter to the statement of Sir
Walter Scott, had the object been to present a surreptitious brooch in
place of the real one. The ornament consists of a circular plate,
about four inches in diameter, having a tongue like that of a common
buckle on the under side. The upper side is magnificently ornamented. First, from the margin rises a neatly-formed rim, with hol-
lows cut in the edge at certain distances, like the embrasures in an
embattled wall. From a circle within this rim rise eight round, taper-
ing obelisks, about an inch and a quarter high, finely cut, and each
studded at top with a river pearl. Within this circle of obelisks there
is a second rim, also ornamented with carved work, and within which

rises a neat circular case, occupying the whole centre of the brooch and slightly overtopping the obelisks. The exterior of this case, instead of forming a plain circle, projects into eight semi-cylinders, which relieve it from all appearance of heaviness. The upper part is likewise carved very elegantly, and in the centre there is a large gem. This case may be taken off, and within there is a hollow which might have contained any small articles upon which a particular value was set.

Barbour does not tell the story of the Brooch of Lorne, and the authenticity of the modern article rests chiefly on the following statement, to be credited, or otherwise, as readers are disposed. For our own part, it seems to us that the traditions relative to the brooch are too numerous and steady to permit us to doubt of the reality of the story; and, whatever scepticism may say, there appears no sound reason for doubting the new-found article to be the veritable antique one. It underwent some odd turns of fortune. In the civil war during the reign of the first Charles, the Macdougal of that day adhered to the royal cause, and suffered as much thereby as he had formerly done by opposing the Bruces. In 1647, he was besieged in Dunolly (the old seat, and still the seat of the house,) by a detachment of General Leslie's troops, under Colonel Montgomery. From the impregnable nature of the situation, he was successful in holding out this strength; but Goalen Castle was taken, sacked and burned. Campbell of Inveraw, who took part in the latter affair, secured the brooch of King Robert, which he took into his possession as fair spoil, though he did not think proper to make his good fortune too well known, lest the Macdougal might have thought it necessary afterwards to attempt the recovery of the highly-valued relic by force. Time rolled on; the Macdougal of the early part of the last century lost his lands in consequence of his embracing the cause of the Pretender in 1715; his son regained them in consequence of keeping loyal in 1745. Meanwhile, the brooch won at Dalree continued safe, amidst all the vicissitudes of the family fortunes, in the strong chest at Inveraw. To the Macdougals themselves it was not even known to exist.

At length, about fifty years ago, this precious relic passed into the hands of a cadet of the Inveraw family, who, at a subsequent time, appointed it by testament to be sold, and the proceeds divided amongst his younger children. It was accordingly, about the year 1819, sent to London to be exposed for sale, the price put upon it being a thousand pounds. The late King George IV., then Prince Regent, is said to have offered five hundred pounds for the brooch, but without obtaining it; nor did any other customer appear who was willing to give the large price put upon it by the possessor. It must be understood that, when thus laid before the public, it was openly described as the *Brooch of Lorne*, originally the property of King Robert Bruce; yet the fact of its existence and exposure for sale did not become known to the representative of the Macdougal family till after it had been withdrawn from the market. Ultimately, in the year 1825, the late amiable General Campbell of Lochnell, being anxious to bestow some mark of grateful regard on his esteemed friend and neighbour, Macdougal, purchased the brooch, and caused it to be presented to that gentleman by his chief, the Duke of Argyll, at a social meeting of the landholders of the county. It thus, after an interval of more than a century and a half, found its way back to the family, who, next to King Robert and his heirs and representatives, were certainly its most rightful owners. It is at present kept with great care at Dunolly Castle.

Colin Campbell, the first Earl of Argyll, was a man of extraordinary talents and great influence. He fully vindicated the dignity of his clan, and extended the territorial possessions of his house. He played an important part in the public life of Scotland, filling the position of High Chancellor of the kingdom under the rule of James III. and James IV. It is hinted by some that his great ambition and success in acquiring lands gave birth to the bye-word "the greed of the Campbells;" but Mr. Hogg, the author previously referred to, gives a more reasonable opinion that "the whole question resolves itself into the fact that he and his generation were men of ability, skilful in detecting and using opportunities after the fashion of their day."

It would be interesting and instructive had we the space at command to sketch the prominent features in the lives of the second, third and fourth Earl of Argyll who followed the first in unbroken male succession from father to son. The great prominence which history accords to the fifth Earl of Argyll, however, demands a passing notice. He had all the advantages of birth of his predecessors, and managed to improve upon these favorable conditions by a series of fortunate marriages which, by a wise policy, were contracted by the house. Through this means he became one of the leading and most powerful peers of the realm in the days of Queen Mary. " He had been educated by John Douglas, the "first Protestant bishop of St. Andrews, and acquired from " him those liberal religious principles which were destined " to throw at once a glory and a gloom on the annals of the " house. The Earl has been variously judged by historians " for his conduct during the reign of the unhappy Queen " Mary. It is unquestionable that he adhered to his reli- " gious principles throughout, or, in other words, to the " Presbyterian party, called the 'Congregation.' He was " twice wedded, but left no children, and was succeeded by " his brother in the year 1575."

Colin, a name often repeated in the history of the clan, the sixth Earl of Argyll, was distinguished alike by political and military successes. He maintained the dignity of the house, and held the position of his predecessors of Lord High Chanceller of Scotland. But his son, Archibald, was a man of still greater talents and influence. At the age of eighteen he was placed at the head of an army, and commanded to lead the power of the west against that of the north. His campaign was a failure, bus it is said that the singular good fortune of his family did not long desert him. " The Macgregors, and the Macdonalds, of Kintyre," says Mr. Hogg, " had broken out into excesses against the peace

"of the realm, and the Earl of Argyll was ordered out for
"their suppression. Here the policy of the Campbells,
"which lay in adhering ever to the Lowland monarchy in
"opposition to the feelings and principles which guided the
"more northern Gael, led to a large acquisition of territory
"by the house of Lochow. Far be it from us to approve of
"the sanguinary treatment too often experienced by the
"'Children of the Mist' (Macgregors), but, in fairness, we
"should look at both sides of the question. The Lowlands
"were gradually settling down into a condition of order and
"quietude, and the incursions of the neighbouring mountain-
"eers constituted a perpetual and heavy grievance. The
"Macgregors, to take them as an example, were located on
"the very borders of the low country, and their predatory
"habits made them a terror and a curse. If any reader of
"romantic temperament should feel displeased at this lan-
"guage, let him recollect what occurred in the very middle
"of the comparatively civilized eighteenth century, when the
"sons of Rob Roy carried off a helpless young woman from
"her friends, and, for the sake of her money, completed the
"abduction by all the horrors of a forced marriage. If
"such things were done so lately, what unheard of outrages
"must have been signalised earlier times! It is not to
"apologise for or justify any wilful cruelties practised on
"such clans as the Macgregors that these things are men-
"tioned, but simply to prove that the picture has two sides.
"Their own practices tended largely to pull down vengeance
"on their heads. In the case now more directly under con-
"sideration, the Earl of Argyll, conjoining his power with
"that of the Gordons, attacked and nearly exterminated the
"unhappy Macgregors. The Macdonalds of Kintyre were
"at the same time reduced and partly expelled. Their

"lands were transferred to Argyll, thus adding another fair portion of the west to his family domains."

Archibald Campbell, eighth Earl and first Marquis of Argyll, introduces us to the great civil wars of the seventeenth century, in which he acted a most brave and gallant part, being equalled only by his great foe, the Marquis of Montrose. Montrose upheld the royal prerogative, while Argyll contended for civil and religious freedom. These two noblemen were the great leaders in Scotland in the war which lost Charles I. his head, and it is difficult to say which deserves most of our admiration for their deeds of chivalry. Montrose may have outstripped his opponent in the brilliancy of his daring, but in the closing scenes of their lives, in the serenity of their dying hours,—both of them perishing on the scaffold—the Marquis of Argyll was, perhaps, the greater hero.

The latter was the leader of the Presbyterian party in Scotland for a considerable period. However, he characterized his acts in such a manner as to be regarded, if not friendly, at least without enmity to royalty or to the house of the Stewarts. But when the King persisted in the most despotic proceedings, he was, at length, forced into a decided opposition, and signed the National Covenant, which created such a breach between the people and the throne. He was the last of the Scotch noblemen who took this step, and it may be fairly doubted whether or not he would have taken such an extreme position, if the King had supplied him with no private reasons. He received personal provocation from the Court of Charles I. of a decided type. On visiting London at the King's request, in 1683, he discovered that the monarch had sanctioned an invasion of the western coast of Scotland by the Irish under Lord Antrim,

STORY OF HOUSE OF ARGYLL. 47

who, because he was a Macdonald, had been promised the estates of Kintyre, so recently accorded to the house of Argyll. This private provocation decided him to join the popular party in the General Assembly in 1638, when the liturgy was condemned, the presbyteries fully re-established, and episcopacy abolished. One year later Charles I. proposed to invade Scotland. It was on this occasion that the Marquis of Argyll raised 900 of his clan to aid in repelling both the King and the invasion from Ireland.

Various attempts at pacification followed, but with few good results, in which the Marquis of Argyll was called on to act against the Earl of Athol and the Ogilvies in the north, and he forced them to submit to the Scottish Parliament.* Montrose, his family foe, was at this time a young man burning for distinction, and, though inclined to favour the popular party, felt deeply irritated by the ascendancy of Argyll. An accusation of disloyalty, brought unadvisedly against the latter by Montrose, only served, by its total failure, to prove that the chief of the Campbells meditated no overthrow of the regal authority. Charles I. seems to have been quite satisfied on this subject. It was on his visit to Scotland in 1641 that he raised Argyll to the dignity of the Marquisate. But the obstinacy of Charles soon precipitated matters in England to a bloody conclusion; and the sympathies of Argyll and the popular party in Scotland were entirely against the arbitrary movements of royalty. For several successive seasons the Marquis was engaged, more or less actively, against Montrose and the other adherents of Charles,.and he had his feelings of hostility aggravated by a cruel incursion of the Irish into

---

*John Hogg's " Clan Campbell," p. 22.

Argyllshire. At length, on the 2d of February, 1645, the forces of Argyll and Montrose met at Inverlochy. The Campbells fought bravely, but could not withstand the skill and daring of the royalist leader. He routed his opponents utterly, and the Marquis of Argyll escaped only by means of a boat on the lake. Candid authors have charged him with pusillanimity on this occasion; but there is so much to counteract the accusation that but few have adopted any such opinion. Soon after the Marquis was again mortified by witnessing a second defeat of the Covenanters at Kilsyth by Montrose; but in another month the great royalist was himself overthrown by Leslie at Philiphaugh. This was in 1645.

But, in the midst of all this bloodshed, the Marquis of Argyll was endeavoring to effect a reconciliation between the King and his subjects. In the interests of such a peace he visited Newcastle, and personally waited on His Majesty. "When Charles put himself into the hands of the Scottish "people," says an English author, "Argyll, to his credit, "took no part in any of the discussions for the disposal of "the royal person. That he did not go further, and oppose "the deliverance of the King to the English Parliament, is "solely excusable on the ground that the best friends of "Charles in the South warned him that Scotland would "have to bear the whole weight of an English war if any "opposition were offered by the Scots to the progress of "events in the South. An attempt, however, was really "made by the northern friends of royalty, and it ended in "a contest equally disastrous and fruitless. Charles I. per- "ished on the scaffold at Whitehall, on the 30th January, "1649. The present remarks are not made with the view "of defending the conduct of the Scots generaliy in deliv-

STORY OF HOUSE OF ARGYLL. 49

"ering up the King—an act scarcely defensible in any point
"of view—but in order, simply, to explain the conduct of
"the Marquis of Argyll. He showed his unabated attach-
"ment to the ancient race of the Scottish kings, by being
"the most active of the nobles in calling Charles II. to the
"throne. He personally crowned the young monarch at
"Scone in 1650. Even after the defeat at Dunbar in the
"same year, he adhered so warmly to the royal cause that
"Charles voluntarily gave him a letter, announcing the in-
"tent to create him Duke of Argyll as soon as circum-
"stances permitted, and also saying, 'Whenever it shall
"'please God to restore me to my just rights, I shall see
"'him paid the £40,000 sterling which is due to him.'
"Such a document as this should put a stop to all charges
"of disloyalty against Argyll. Nor can we believe such
"accusations because, on the failure of Charles II. at
"Worcester, and his consequent expulsion from Britain,
"the Marquis, being brought a prisoner from Inverary to
"Edinburgh, admitted the authority of Cromwell's govern-
"ment. For this compulsory submission to a power which
"all Britain at the time, through love or fear, obeyed, the
"ungrateful prince, when restored to the throne in 1660,
"brought the Marquis of Argyll to the scaffold, probably
"deeming it the easiest way of repaying the £40,000
"which were due to him. Argyll had gone to London to
"acknowledge and welcome Charles, but the King would
"not see him, and sent him back a prisoner to Scotland.
"Being there placed on his trial, the indictment, consisting
"of fourteen different charges, comprehended a narrative
"of the whole transactions in Scotland, from the first op-
"position to the King till its final subjugation under Crom-
"well. But the whole of the charges were so ridiculous as

" to be almost ineffective; and the Court, although evi-
" dently with great reluctance, were compelled to exonerate
" Argyll from all blame in the matter of the execution of
" Charles. The crown lawyers, thus baffled, were at length
" obliged to rest their case on the *compliance* of Argyll
" with the English during Cromwell's usurpation, as the
" only ground on which a charge of treason could be rested.
" On such a charge as this, if held to be a capital crime,
" half the population of Britain deserved hanging, and
" the first man of all honoured with the rope should
" have been General Monk. Argyll, in an extemporaneous
" reply, expressed the joy he felt at the restoration of his
" majesty, and enumerating the services he had performed,
" and the marks of favour he had received, both from him
" and his royal father, desired the Parliament to consider
" how unlikely it was that he should have ever harboured
" a thought to their disadvantage. With Paul, in another case,
" he might say, the things alleged against him could not be
" proven; but this he would confess, that, in the way al-
" lowed by solemn oaths and covenants, he served his God,
" his country and his king. He entreated those who were
" capable of understanding, when those things now charged
" upon him as crimes were enacted, to recollect the state of
" the kingdom, the circumstances of the crime, and how
" both themselves and others were carried irresistibly
" along by the current of events without any rebellious
" intentions; besides, he had been among the last that
" had entered into the confederacy and taken the coven-
" ants. The transactions of public bodies, or of officers act-
" ing under the authority of the State, had never been held
" treason, nor was he responsible in his individual capacity,
" for all the deeds of that party to which he belonged. The

" cruelties alleged to have been committed by his clan, he
" averred were greatly exaggerated, yet unhappily too well
" justified, by the terrible devastation to which their district
" had been repeatedly exposed; and the extent of their own
" previous calamity would extenuate, if it did not exculpate,
" the crime; but, be that as it might, the blame could never
" attach to him, who was in England when the alleged cruel-
" ties took place. The surrender of the king was the act of
" a parliament at which he was not so much as present; nor
" was there the shadow of proof that he ever advised the
" death of his sacred majesty—an execrable deed at which
" he had ever expressed his abhorrence, and for which,
" could the smallest evidence be adduced, he should ask no
" mercy. He could acquit himself of disloyalty, even in
" thought; and for whatever other error or fault he might
" have been guilty previously to the year 1651, he pleaded
" his majesty's indemnity, granted in the parliament at
" Perth that year. As to what was done by him under the
" usurpers, they were common compliances, in which all the
" kingdom equally shared, and for which many had the
" sanction of the king himself—who declared that he thought
" it prudence, and not rebellion, for honest men to preserve
" their estates from ruin, and reserve themselves till God
" should show some probable way for his return. Among
" all who complied passively, none was less favoured than
" himself; what he did was really in self-defence. And how
" could I suppose, he added, that I was acting criminally,
" when the learned gentleman, who now acts as his majesty's
" advocate, took the same oaths to the commonwealth as
" myself. The Lord Advocate (Sir John Fletcher), who
" could not rebut the force of such an appeal, endeavoured
" to weaken its influence by the most unseemly interrup-

"tions. To these the Marquis meekly replied, that he had "learned in the school of adversity to suffer reproach."

The trial of the Marquis of Argyll not only produced a general belief in his innocence of the crimes laid to his charge, but evinced his superior ability and heroic courage. Thus runs the story of his trial and execution :—

Two sons of the Marquis, Lord Lorne and Lord Neil Campbell, were in London, exerting their influence in their father's behalf. The Scottish parliament finding their evidence defective, despatched the Earls of Glencairn and Rothes to the English court, with an application to General Monk for advice. The Scottish parliament being again met to consider the whole case, and appearances being strongly in favor of the Marquis, a messenger, who had come express from London, knocked violently at the door of the parliament house. Upon his admission he presented a packet to the commissioner, which everyone concluded contained a remission, or some other warrant in favour of the Marquis, especially as the bearer was a Campbell. But upon the packet being opened, to the amazement of Argyll's friends, it was found to consist of a great many letters addressed by his lordship to Monk, while he was Governor of Scotland, and which with unparalleled baseness he had reserved, to see if they were absolutely necessary; and having been informed by the commissioner's envoys of the scantiness of the proof, he had sent post by an especial courier. The letters were decisive as to the fact of *compliance* with the usurpers—that is, of Argyll being a *passive*, while Monk himself had been an *active* agent; and on this ground alone was the Marquis found guilty of treason by a majority of a parliament almost all of whom were more culpable than he was. Argyll was condemned to death, and on the occasion the young Lord of Montrose, now restored to the honours of his ancestors, refused to give a vote, thus repaying the chief of the Campbells for his forbearance in declining to assent (in 1650) to the execution of the great Marquis of Montrose.

The manner of his being executed being put to the vote,

"hang or head," it was carried that he should be beheaded, and that his head should be placed on the same pinnacle, at the end of the Tolbooth, where Montrose's had been formerly fixed. Sentence was pronounced against him on the 25th May, 1661, and ordered to be carried into execution on the 27th, at the Cross of Edinburgh. From the hour of his condemnation the Marquis of Argyll behaved in a way worthy of the head of the Scottish Presbyterians. The inhuman speed evinced by his foes did not appal the Marquis. He received his sentence kneeling, which was pronounced by the Earl of Crawford. On rising, he only remarked, "I set the crown on his Majesty's head, and now he hastens me to a better crown than his own." The parliament seemed much affected with this sad instance of mutability of fortune, and his lordship's humble, composed demeanour drew tears even from his enemies; yet, when he requested a delay of only ten days, till his sentence should be communicated to the King, they, with the inconsistency and inhumanity so common among collective bodies, refused him the respite, and sent him to the common jail among the ordinary prisoners for the last two days they allowed him to prepare for death.

The Marchioness was waiting for him in the Tolbooth, to whom the Marquis said as he entered, "they have given me till Monday to be with you, my dear; therefore, let us improve it." She, embracing him, wept bitterly, and in agony exclaimed, "the Lord will requite it!" "the Lord will requite it!" Calm and composed, he replied, "forbear; truly I pity them; they know not what they are doing; they may shut me in where they please, but they cannot shut out God from me. For my part I am as content to be here as in the castle, and as content in the castle as in the Tower of London, and as content there as when at liberty, and I hope to be as content on the scaffold as in any of them all." He spent the Sunday not only calmly but cheerfully, in exercises of devotion, with several ministers who were permitted to attend him, to whom he remarked that he was naturally of a timorous disposition, and bade them observe how wonderfully he was delivered from all fear. At his own desire, the Marchioness took leave of him on Sunday night, after which he passed some hours in uninterrupted and pleasant sleep. It is said that one of the most adverse of his judges came to see him on the night before his death, and was so much struck to find him sleeping with the utmost calmness, as to retire from the scene with feelings of the deepest perturbation. On the morning of Monday he wrote a letter to the king, asserting his innocence, recommending his widow and family to his Majesty's protection, and requesting that his just debts might be allowed to be paid out of his estate. He dined with his friends precisely at twelve o'clock, after which he retired for prayer, and on rejoining the company, appeared in an ecstacy of joy. As he was quitting the jail, he observed to some of his fellow prisoners whom he was leaving, "I could die like a Roman, but I choose rather to die like a Christian." He was accompanied to the place of execution by several noblemen and gentlemen in mourning, with whom he walked steadily down the street in a very solemn but undaunted manner; and mounting the scafford with the greatest serenity, saluted all who were upon it In a speech delivered without a falter, he forgave his enemies and vindicated his own conduct, which, at that awful moment, he declared had never been influenced by any motives of self-aggrandisement or disloyalty. He had been cordial, he said in his desire to bring the king home, and in his endeavours for him to be at home; nor had he ever corresponded with his enemies during the time he was in the country. But he warned those who, if their private interest went well, cared not whether religion sank or swam, and accounted it rebellion to adhere to their covenant engagements to beware how they deceived themselves; that no magistrate could absolve them from the oath to God; that religion must be a main and not a secondary object; and that they were the best subjects who were the best Christians. The times, he added, were likely to prove very sinning times or very suffering times, and let Christians make their choice; there was a sad dilemma in the business, sin and suffer ; and, truly, he that would choose the better part would choose to suffer. Having again spent some time in devotion, when he had finished, he had distributed some last tokens of remembrance to the friends who were with him. After his doubtlet was off, and immediately before he laid his head on the block, he addressed those near him—" Gentlemen, I desire you, and all that hear me, again to take notice and remember that now, when I am entering into eternity, and to appear before my Judge, and as I desire salvation, and expect eternal happiness from Him, I am free from any accession, by knowledge, contriving, counsel, or any ways, of his late majesty's death; and I pray the Lord to preserve the present king, and to pour out His best blessings upon his person and government, and the Lord give him good and faithful counsellors." He then knelt down and at a given signal—the lifting up of his hand—the knife of the maiden* severed his head from his body. According to the sentence, his head was affixed on the Tolbooth, but his body was given to his friends, by whom it was carried, with a numerous attendance, in funeral procession to Kilpatrick, thence transported by water to Dunoon, and finally deposited with honor in the family burying-place at Kilmure. Fortunately, those who persecuted this nobleman to death were not, as was too frequently then the case, rewarded with his honors and estates. Through the intercession of Lauderdale, Lord Lorne succeeded to the estates of his father and all the titles, except that of marquis.

The son and successor of the Marquis of Argyll, Archibald Campbell, shared in his father's troubles, and lay in prison for a considerable time under sentence of death. But in June, 1663, he was liberated and soon obtained his grandfather's title of Earl of Argyll, with the estates of the house. Thus again at least a part of their former

---

*The instrument called the Maiden was introduced by the Regent, Earl of Morton, and is still preserved as a relic in the Museum of the Scottish Antiquaries. It is a simple form of the French guillotine.

glory returned to the Campbells. The policy of adhering to the constitution was kept up by the Earl of Argyll, and it was to him that "letters of fire and sword" against the Macleans were entrusted in 1678. As a privy-counsellor, a commissioner of the treasury, and an extraordinary lord of session, Argyll acted until James, Duke of York, afterwards king, came down to Scotland. The Earl was now exposed to great danger from his unwillingness to take the *test*, or oath regarding the terms of succession to the throne; and when he really took the test, he put the following protest on record in the books of Parliament: "I think no man can explain this oath but for himself. Accordingly, I take it, as far as it is consistent with itself and the Protestant religion." The bearing of this explanation against the Catholic heir to the throne was too obvious to be tolerated by that personage, and after communication with Charles II., Argyll was committed to custody in the Castle of Edinburgh. His father had resigned into the hands of royalty the Justiciaryship of Scotland, hereditary in the family; but the heritable jurisdiction of Argyllshire still remained in the house, and it was sought to take away this privilege, with part of the estates. The malice of the court, or rather of the Duke of York, brought the Earl of Argyll to the bar of the Justiciary Court in December, 1681; and the King's advocate, Mackenzie, a man so singularly marked by perverted talents, did his utmost to implicate the Earl in the crime of treason on the score of the "explanation" given of the test. The judges were closely divided in opinion, and to solve the difficulty, the court brought in Lord Nairn, a judge long superannuated. He was roused from his bed at midnight, and, as he knew nothing that had passed, the proceedings were read over again in his presence.

STORY OF HOUSE OF ARGYLL. 57

He was found to have fallen sound asleep when called on for his vote. It was decided against Argyll; and, unlike his father, the Marquis of Montrose (grandson of the great Montrose) sat as foreman or chancellor on the condemnatory jury. The conviction was a capital one—for leasing-making and high treason.*

But the courage of a woman saved Argyll on this occasion from his impending fate. Lady Sophia Lindsay, his daughter-in-law, visited him in the castle before his removal to the prison of the condemned, and had the address to get him safely forth in the guise of a page, holding up her train. The Earl passed over to Holland; but a circumstance occurred before that time which shows that the Duke of York was his true enemy. Argyll had not yet left Britain, when an offer was made to Charles II. to point out where he might be found. "Pooh! pooh!" cried the King, "hunt a hunted partridge! for shame!" This one quality of good-nature has long excused many blunders on the part of Charles—nay, many vices, many crimes. But of this point we are not called on here to judge.*

When the Earl of Argyll moved from Holland on the death of Charles II., he was only a few years ahead of the times. He undertook what was successfully carried out three years later by the revolution of 1688. He sacrificed himself, as has been well said, as the avant-courier of a permanent change in the British Monarchy. It was in May, 1685, that the Earl of Argyll left Holland with a body of his friends, and attempted to increase his forces from his former supporters in the west Highlands. But, as we have

---

*John Hogg, Esq., London, Eng., in Clan Campbell.

said, he was in advance of the feeling of the country. The acts of James VII. had not yet been fully developed or understood. From these and other causes the nobleman found himself without supporters—nay, forsaken by those whom he had a right to expect would be the last to leave his ranks. But, in the midst of these difficulties, Argyll determined to fight his enemies whenever and wherever he could find them. In this determination he suffered the further opposition of his officers. A march was attempted towards Glasgow; but, through the stupidity of his guides, he was led into moors, and lost his baggage in morasses. Finally, being reduced to a force of five hundred, his forces disbanded, and the Earl, in the disguise of a countryman, was wounded and taken prisoner. In this unfortunate hour he revealed his rank by an unguarded exclamation. This knowledge of his rank, while it elicited the warmest sympathy of his captors, made it the more important that he should be imprisoned there. On the 20th of June, 1685, he was conducted to the Castle of Edinburgh, with his hands fastened behind his back, preceded by the public execution. Here he was put to death ten days later, bearing his fate with the great courage and calmness for which his family are so justly celebrated. In his last hours, face to face with his cruel fate, he wrote his own epitaph, and, while we may not expect even an Earl to be very poetical under such circumstances, yet, as Horace Walpole says, there is an heroic satisfaction of conscience expressed in the lines worthy of the cause in which he fell. Some of the lines are prophetic of the revolution of 1688, and show that the Earl of Argyll was acting on the broadest principles of patriotism and loyalty:—

> "On my attempt though Providence did frown,
> His oppressed people God at length shall own;
> Another hand, with more successful speed,
> Shall raise the remnant, bruise the serpent's head.
> Though my head fall, that is no tragic story,
> Since, going hence, I enter endless glory."

There is one thing to be cited in proof of the uncertainty of political issues in these times, and that is, that while Argyll and Montrose pursued directly opposite courses during their active lives, they both came at last to the scaffold with composure and songs of heroic triumph. The forces which followed Argyll to carry out what, in a certain sense, he undertook, soon made their appearance under William of Orange. His victories have been already often told. King William did not forget the Campbells, but one of his first acts was to restore the house of Argyll. Archibald Campbell, the heir to the house, was put into possession and enjoyment of the family honors, and not only this, but raised to dignities which his predecessors did not enjoy. He was elevated to the highest offices of state in Scotland, and was finally created DUKE OF ARGYLL, in June, 1701. He became a favorite with William III., and during his reign raised a regiment almost entirely of his own name, who did heroic service in the wars in Flanders. Archibald Campbell, the first Duke of Argyll, Marquis of Lorne and Earl of Campbell, died in September, 1703. This event introduces us to one of the most eminent leaders of the house of Argyll, viz., JOHN, DUKE OF ARGYLL AND GREENWICH. Pope, who never flatters, spoke of this nobleman in no meagre praise:—

> "Argyll, the state's whole thunder born to wield,
> And shake alike the senate and the field."

Before coming into possession of the Dukedom he had distinguished himself at the head of a regiment in Flanders, under King William, while yet a mere youth. Before he had reached the age of twenty-five he was made an extraordinary lord of session and a privy-councillor. At the age of twenty-seven he was made Lord High Commissioner to the Scottish Parliament, the Court, it is said, being actuated in his appointment by the high promise of his character, his vast patrimonial possessions, and the great general influence of his family in Scotland. On this occasion he made considerable display. "Forty coaches and six
" hundred horsemen met him on his approach to Edin-
" burgh, and thus was he ushered in triumph, as Lord Com-
" missioner, into the ancient royalty. A very handsome
" person, and a demeanor manly and staid beyond his
" years, contributed, with his other advantages, to render
" him, at the time, by far the most popular of all the mag-
" nates of Scotland. In his opening speech to Parliament,
" his Grace recommended the settlement of the succession
" to the throne in the Protestant line, and advocated a
" Treaty of Union with England. Having performed his
" duties in Scotland, and procured the appointment of proper
" parties to discuss the terms of the Union, the Duke was
" led, by his active spirit, to join the army of Marlborough
" in Flanders. At Ostend and Menin he distinguished him-
" self highly, and entered the latter place as the leader of
" the victors. He returned to his own country to assist in
" carrying out the treaty of union, and braved much un-
" popularity in accomplishing that great object, which
" nearly all men now acknowledge to have saved North
" and South Britain from endless feuds. As colonel of the
" third regiment of foot, his Grace acted an important part

" in Flanders, whither he returned betwixt the years 1707
" and 1710, being raised to such a rank, and entrusted with
" such commands, as befitted his pretensions and merits.
" At the battle of Oudenarde, and at the sieges of Lisle,
" Ghent, and Tournay, he made himself peculiarly eminent;
" and at Malplaquet, where victory seemed about to desert
" the British arms, he exposed himself so fearlessly that
" his clothes were penetrated by a number of balls, though
" his person escaped unharmed. The Duke of Marlborough
" esteemed and employed Argyll, though the very high
" rank and talents of the latter seem to have bred a jealousy
" betwixt the two, and frequently to have set them at vari-
" ance. The Duke of Argyll returned to Britain in 1710.
" It is by no means to his honour that he then opposed the
" motion in the House of Lords for thanking Marlborough,
" though Harley (afterwards Earl of Oxford) and other
" enemies of the conqueror of Blenheim were delighted by
" the proceeding. Their influence gave to Argyll an oppor-
" tunity of rivalling his late superior, by his being em-
" ployed as commander-in-chief of the British forces then
" acting in Spain. His Grace arrived in Barcelona in May,
" 1711, but he found the troops in a condition miserably
" unfit for service. He called for money and aid from
" home; his call was unheeded. The anxiety of his mind
" brought on a severe illness, and on recovering from it, he
" had the mortification to be compelled to quit Spain with
" all his forces. Undoubtedly, however, the failure of
" assistance from home in men and means was to a great
" extent the cause of these reverses—the more galling, it
" may be supposed, from the unvarying successes of the
" Duke of Marlborough.

" Soured in temper by the bad treatment which he im-

" agined himself to have experienced at the hands of the
" home government, the Duke of Argyll, on his return to
" Britain, joined the party of the opposition in Parliament,
" and even voted for a repeal of the act of union. His plea
" was, that the Protestant succession was now safe without
" that treaty; and he proved himself to be so far sincere by
" furthering and securing the interests of the. Elector of
" Hanover. All along the principles of his family had been
" favourable to the Whig party—in short to moderate liber-
" alism as opposed to the high Jacobite or ultramonarchical
" ideas of other statesmen of the seventeenth and eighteenth
" centuries. He did not deviate from these principles in
" his present movements. The result of all was, that
" George I. looked on Argyll as the main pillar of his power
" in Scotland, at the time when Queen Anne died and left
" the throne vacant for his ascension. The Duke was
" named commander of the forces in the north in September
" 1714; and when the Earl of Mar appeared in rebellion
" during the following year, his Grace was ordered out
" against the insurgents. He found the military power of
" the crown in Scotland in a state of wretched weakness, but
" he led the troops under his command against the Earl of
" Mar, and met him at Sheriffmuir, near Dunblane, on the
" 15th of November, 1715. Both lay upon their arms all
" night, and a stone is still shown on the site of the High-
" landers' bivouac, indented all round with marks occasioned
" by the broad-swords of those warriors who here sharpened
" their weapons for the next day's conflict. The Highlanders
" had come down from their fastnesses, with a resolution to
" fight as their ancestors had fought at Kilsyth and Killie-
" crankie. Their enthusiasm may be guessed from the
" following anecdote. A Lowland gentleman observing

"amongst their bands a man of ninety years of age from the
"upper part of Aberdeenshire, had the curiosity to ask how
"one so aged, and seemingly so feeble, had thought of join-
"ing this enterprise. The old man, laying his hand on a
"pistol which he carried in his bosom, replied, 'I have sons
"here, sir, and I have grandsons, if they fail to do their
"duty can I not shoot them!' The attack of these resolute
"soldiers upon the left wing of the royal army was irresisti-
"ble. The chief of Clanranald was killed as they were ad-
"vancing, but instead of damping their ardour, this only
"served to inspire them with greater fury. 'To-morrow
"for lamentation!' cried the young chieftain of Glengary,
"'To-day for revenge!' The battle undoubtedly checked
"the rebel army and broke up their plans; but to pronounce
"who gained the victory has puzzled historian and poet
"ever since. 'Some say that we wan and some say that
"they wan,' has been ever the cry of the Scots in speaking
"of that engagement; and even Robert Burns thought the
"dilemma worthy of a spirit-stirring, though semi-humorous
"lyric. Argyll himself is said to have turned poet on the
"occasion, but it may be doubted whether he did not mere-
"ly content himself with making use of the old catch verse
"of the 'Bob o'Dunblane'—'If it be na weel bobbit, we'll bob
"it again."

His Grace was so far victorious as to check the advance
of the insurgents southwards. Indeed they were never after
able to make a formidable stand against the royal army.
Early in 1716 the Duke moved northwards towards Perth,
but the army of Lord Mar had disbanded, and he, with
other chiefs, had sought hiding places. When His Grace
visited London he advocated the most lenient treatment of
the Highland chieftians, by which he gained the great dis-

pleasure of the King and court. In this course he proved his own wisdom, for had his advice been accepted, there would have been no civil war of 1745.

But there was another circumstance which placed the Duke in opposition to the Court, which, together with a sketch of His Grace's life, is related by Mr. Hogg:—

From the days of Henry IV. to those of George III. the heirs-apparent of the British monarchs had almost always been placed in an attitude of hostility to their sires, chiefly because the rising sun is apt to attract worshippers, and to lessen the homage paid to and expected by the setting luminary. A party of the young and active in the state invariably congregated around the sovereign *in posse*, and hence arose the jealousy of the sovereign *in esse*. Our past annals abound with evidences of this truth. In the present instance the Duke of Argyll chanced to acquire the especial favour of the Prince of Wales, and, in proportion, lost that of the King. In 1716, he was deprived of all his employments about the royal household, and it was not till 1719 that he was fully restored to favour. In that year he was created High Steward, and received the title of DUKE of GREENWICH, having before sat in the English Parliament as Earl of Greenwich. He was one of those well-meaning patriots who proposed the limitation of the number of English peers, and the augmentation of the roll of Scottish representative nobles from sixteen to twenty-five. He failed in his object at the time; but, by the conference of British titles on Scottish barons, his design of equalization has since been carried out fully. He strenuously fulfilled his duties in parliament during the busy years succeeding 1715, and was always at hand to defend there the interests of his own northern land. He held but a dubious position with the court, but the Chief of the Campbells was of too much importance to be pushed to the wall by any changes of men or measures. When the famous Porteous riot took place in Edinburgh, his Grace courageously stood forth to check the wild retaliatory steps which it was proposed to take against the city of Edinburgh. It was then, on being taunted with interested motives, that he pronounced the speech which Sir Walter Scott has rendered familiar to all general readers, by quoting it in the "Heart of Midlothian:"—"I am no minister, I never was a minister, and I never will be one. I thank God I had always too great a value for those few abilities which nature has given to me, to employ them in doing any drudgery, or any *job* of any kind whatever." In short, the Duke punished his ministerial opponents unparingly in his oration, and frightened them into milder measures with respect to the city of Edinburgh. It was on this occasion also, that he is said to have risked his head in imparting a similar lesson to royalty. Queen Caroline, left regent at the time of the Porteous mob by her royal lord's absence in Hanover, indignantly declared to the Duke that "she would turn Scotland into a hunting-seat." "If that be the case, madam," said his Grace, coolly, "I must go down and prepare my hounds." The threat was courteously worded, but was in reality a terrible one; and the Queen felt its true force. She was guilty of no further ebullitions of anger of the same kind. Edinburgh was pardoned on payment of a fine.

The Duke of Argyll opposed the conduct of Sir Robert Walpole and the Duke of Newcastle in parliament with energy, and, in 1742, Walpole resigned the premiership. But though the command of the British army was given to Argyll, he was unable to reconcile himself to other appointments made, and held his place but for a few days. Perhaps ill-health had some share in this proceeding. He died at all events soon afterwards (4th of October, 1743), in the sixty-fifth year of his age. He was interred in Westminster Abbey, and the talents of Roubiliac were exerted in erecting a beautiful monument to his memory, still to be seen in the southern transept of the edifice.

There must have been something truly grand, on the whole, in the character of John, Duke of Argyll and Greenwich, whose career has now been thus briefly traced. No common personage could have drawn forth the praises which

Pope and Thomson lavished on his head. The commendations of such men involved in them the boon of immortality. The bard of the Seasons says that Scotland beheld in Argyll—

> "Her every virtue, every grace combined,
> Her genius, wisdom, her engaging turn,
> Her pride of honour and her courage tried,
> Calm and intrepid, in the very throat
> Of sulphurous war, on Tenier's dreadful field.
> Nor less the palm of peace enwreathes thy brow ;
> For, powerful as thy sword, from thy rich tongue
> Persuasion flows, and wins the high debate."

There was much silly flattery of the great in the verse of those days, but Pope and Thomson cannot be viewed as common rhyming adulators. The character given by them of the Duke of Argyll may be taken as indicating their real feelings, even admitting that lofty rank so far impressed them as well as others.

By the death of the Duke, his British title of Greenwich became extinct, as he left no male heirs. A considerable portion of his property, though not the Highland estates, went to the Buccleuch family, whose heir had married his daughter, Lady Caroline. The dukedom of Argyll passed to his brother, ARCHIBALD, EARL OF ISLAY, so created previously, for his long and active services to the crown in Scotland. One cannot now help feeling amazed at the rapid transition from camp to court—from the field to the bench —which the habits of that age permitted, and which the lives of the second and third Dukes of Argyll so strikingly exemplified. After serving under Marlborough, the immediate subject of our notice (Duke Archibald finally) returned to Scotland, was appointed Lord High Treasurer there, and as such, aided largely in carrying out the union. For his services, as stated, he was created Earl of Islay. He continued to occupy various high and not unlucrative situations in Scotland up to the outbreak of the Mar rebellion of 1715, when he received several serious wounds at Sheriffmuir, having there joined his brother's army. The offices of High

STORY OF HOUSE OF ARGYLL. 67

Treasurer, Lord Clerk-Registrar, and Keeper of the Privy Seal and the Great Seal, rewarded him successively for his undeviating fidelity to the house of Hanover, and his utility, also, to its ministers—on which latter score he was sometimes at serious variance with his elder brother, then Duke. The Earl of Islay was long the most trusted friend of Sir Robert Walpole in Scotland, and changed not his creed even when his Grace of Argyll was most strenuous in his opposition to that statesman.

It was in 1743, that Archibald Campbell, Earl of Islay, succeeded as Duke of Argyll. Four years later the Jurisdiction-Act called on the Argyll family to part with several important privileges, among which were the hereditary Justice-Generalship and the office of Sheriff. The sum of £21,000 was, however, given as an indemnity.*

---

*It makes one shudder, it may be remarked, to think that, in reality, this transaction was equivalent to the buying away from one man of rank of the power of life and death over all around him. How he and his predecessors wielded it, is not the point here under consideration; but certainly the Lords of Argyll, however, had the *legal* right to do almost anything they chose in their own district, and the withdrawal of such license from their hands could not but be a blessing to the whole country. We may smile at the story of Janet telling her husband to ascend the gallows-tree, "like a man, to please the laird," but the state of society which permitted such scenes is one never to be witnessed again, it is to be hoped, in these islands. There was doubtless a counterbalancing advantage, in so far as the chiefs could often act where the regular laws might have been ineffective; but the good could never equal the evil. The abolition of hereditary jurisdictions was indeed the most important of all the steps taken after the rebellion for the civilization of the Highlands; and we owe it mainly to Duncan Forbes, Lord-President of the Court of Sessions. He was most scurvily recompensed at the time for his patriotic exertions by the government of England. The measures which he suggested, nevertheless, and carried through, were of much more importance to the Gael themselves than to any other parties. He rendered them for the first time comparatively free agents, and gave to them the ordinary privileges of social life. They were no longer liable to be strung up to a tree for refusing to plunder or to fight at the command of the lords of the soil. Yet some very recent writers speak of the willingness to do such acts as—" devotion to the chief," and " romantic fidelity," and by twenty such names and phrases, lamenting the changed state of things. Highly as we respect the character

Duncan Forbes has been justly credited with effecting the needed abolition of hereditary jurisdictions, but it is recorded of the third Duke of Argyll (Archibald, previously Earl of Islay) that he supported the Government in this and all other Scottish measures. He warmly seconded the Lord President's efforts in a plan for employing the young men of the Highlands abroad in the armies.

The third Duke of Argyll was an ardent lover of literature. He founded a magnificent library in the Castle of Inverary. This castle, which was principally erected by his Grace, is situated in Argyllshire in the western Highlands of Scotland, has formed the chief residence of the heads of the Argyll family since the fourteenth century. Inverary, which was constituted a royal burgh by Charles I., is a little over a hundred miles west by north of Edinburgh, and about sixty miles north-west from Glasgow. In front of the town is a small bay of Loch Fyne, surrounded by romantic hills, covered with wood; and on its north side, amid extensive and beautiful grounds, stands the castle. The old building stood at a little distance from the present magnificent ducal mansion, the erection of which was commenced by Archibald, third duke, in 1745, although not finished till several years afterwards. The Castle, an embattled edifice of two storeys over a sunk floor, flanked with round overtopping towers, and surmounted by a square winged pavilion, is built of blue granite. The entrance hall, rising the whole height of the house, is fitted up as an armoury, and

---

of the Highlanders, we believe that many of them would fain have inhabited their hills in quiet of old as now, and that the unhappy ambition and quarrels of the chiefs, who had over every man of them the power of life and death, influenced their actions much more largely than fanciful novelists have been accustomed to allow. Sir Walter Scott knew all this well, though he valued the Gael highly.

contains 150 stand of arms. A spacious gallery leads to the various apartments which are furnished in the most princely style. The paintings and tapestry are of great value. The drives and walks are singularly romantic, and cover, it is said, thirty miles in circumference. At different periods the improvements and decorations on the estate are estimated to have cost £300,000.

His Grace died in April 1761, leaving no family behind him; hence his personal honors as "Earl of Islay and Lord Oransay" became extinct. The Dukedom of Argyll passed to the leneal male heir, son of the Honorable John Campbell of Mamore, second son of Archibald, ninth Earl of Argyll. Thus John Campbell (the second) of Mamore, became the fourth Duke of Argyll in 1761. It is recorded of him that " he was an active man during his career; and, " besides serving in a high military capacity at Dettingen " and elsewhere, he sat in the British House of Commons " during the greatest part of his life, being advanced in " years before he succeeded to the dukedom. He shared " freely in those honours and employments with which the " English ministers ever endeavoured of old to conciliate " the house of Argyll, and maintain their Scottish influence. " His grace enjoyed his title but a few years, dying in Lon-" don in 1770, at the age of seventy-seven."

Another John, his eldest son, inherited the honors and became the fifth Duke of Argyll. " He sat in the House of " Commons before his accession, and also in the House of " Lords, being created LORD SUNDRIDGE (in 1766) whileh is " father lived. It is by the tenure of this baronial title that " the heads of the Campbells still sit among the British " peers. But it was as a soldier that John, Duke of Argyll, " was chiefly distinguished through life. He served in the

"last Scottish civil war, and also on the continent. He
" passed through every grade of military rank in succes-
" sion, and finally became field-marshal of the forces in
" 1796. His career was useful though not brilliant. It should
" be observed, to his honour, that his tenantry, the most
" numerous at the time in Scotland, were the objects of his
" peculiar care when he came to his estates; and he was
" the first President of the Highland Society, that great
" association to which Scottish agriculture and Scottish
" agriculturists are so deeply indebted. He married,
" in 1759, the Duchess Dowager of Hamilton, by birth
" Elizabeth Gunning, one of the most renowned beauties of
" her time, and sister to other ladies scarcely less cele-
" brated for their charms. The family of the Gunnings, who
" were from Ireland, was of itself sufficiently respectable;
" but to their personal attractions were these sisters indebt-
" ed for the high matches made by one and all of them.
" Elizabeth sat in her day as mistress of two of the noblest
" dwellings of Scotland, being successively Duchess of
" Hamilton and Argyll; and the sovereign of the land even
" gave to her the personal title (in 1776) of Baroness Hamil-
" ton, which on the failure of her male issue by the first
" marriage, descended to her children by the Duke of
" Argyll, and is yet a title of the Campbell House. John,
" fifth Duke of Argyll, died at Inverary Castle in 1806."

George William Campbell, eldest surviving son of the fifth Duke of Argyll became the sixth duke. He was married in 1810 to Caroline Elizabeth, daughter of the Earl of Jersey, whose previous union with Lord Paget (afterwards Marquis of Anglesay) had been dissolved in the Scottish courts. His grace died in 1839.

Lord John Douglass-Edward-Henry Campbell, brother to

the sixth Duke of Argyll, became the seventh Duke. "His
" Lordship long held a seat in the Commons' House of
" Parliament, and followed generally the same political
" principles which had caused the Campbell family ever to
" be regarded as a main pillar of the Whig party among the
" nobles of Scotland. The gradual concentration of all official
" business in the British metropolis, however, had long before
" shorn the highest northern peers of much of their im-
" portance, and the abolition of almost all their hereditary
" privileges has greatly changed their position even at
" home. Once on a time a Duke of Argyll never could be
" anything else than a man of the first consequence; now-a-
" days, his repute and influence must rest mainly on his own
" personal qualities and exertions. This change in the
" state of matters was inevitable, as well as others; and the
" disadvantages attending the period of transition should be
" looked to and cared for, as forming the only real source of
" regret and trouble."

The seventh Duke of Argyll died in April, 1847, and was succeeded by his only son, GEORGE DOUGLASS, eighth Duke of Argyll. His Grace still presides over the honours and estates of the Campbell chieftains. "While Marquis of
" Lorne he espoused, on the 31st of July, 1844, the Lady
" Elizabeth Georgiana Sutherland Leveson Gower, eldest
" daughter of George Granville, second Duke of Suther-
" land, and has issue by that marriage—besides a younger
" family of four sons and seven daughters—George-Edward-
" Henry-Douglas-Sutherland, MARQUIS OF LORNE, heir-ap-
" parent to the titles and estates."

In view of the marriage of the Marquis to Her Royal Highness, the Princess Louise, by which the great fortunes of the house of Argyll are to reach their grandest culmination, we will give the honours of the house in full: His Grace is Duke and Earl of Argyll, Marquis of Lorne and Kintyre, Earl of Campbell and Cowal, Viscount of Lochow and Glenilla, Baron Campbell, and Baron of Lorne, Inverary, Mull, Morven, and Tiry, in the peerage of Scotland; and Baron of Sundridge and Hamilton, in the peerage of Great Britain. He is a Knight of the Thistle, a Privy Councillor (1853), Lord Lieutenant and Hereditary Sheriff of the county of Argyll; Hereditary Master of the Queen's Household, Keeper of the Great Seal, and one of Her Majesty's State Counsellors, for Scotland; Admiral of the Western Isles; Keeper of Dunoon Castle, and of Dunstaffnage and Carrick; Chancellor of the University of St. Andrews (1851); a sometime Lord Rector of the University of Glasgow (1854), and President of the Royal Society of Edinburgh (1861); LL.D., Cambridge (1862); a Trustee of the British Museum; and a sometime holder of various political offices.

His Grace, the present Duke of Argyll, was born on the 30th of April, 1823. Before completing his majority, he gave evidence of possessing great ability. At the age of nineteen he attracted considerable attention by the publication of a "Letter to the Peers by a Peer's Son," in which he treated of the Auohterarder case, celebrated as that which led, in 1843, to the disruption of the Church of Scotland and the formation of the Free Kirk. His treatment of this subject was characterized by great ability. His riper studies of ecclesiastical questions resulted in the production, in 1848, of his important work, entitled "Presbytery examined: An Essay, Critical and Historical, on the Ecclesiastical History of Scotland, since the Reformation," the great object of which, as stated in his own words, was

"to give a comprehensive sketch of the principles and tendencies of the Scottish Reformation; to distinguish those which are primary and essential from those which, being the growth of accidental circumstances, are local in their origin, and as local in their meaning; and especially to point out the value of the former in the existing controversies of the Christian Church. In drawing up such a view, and presenting it to the English public, it is right to acknowledge that, as a Presbyterian I cannot pretend to be free from that influence which personal and family associations must always, more or less, exert. But it is not such as would be written by a mere partisan of Presbytery."*
Since his accession to the family honours, his Grace has given many proofs of considerable oratorical ability in the House of Peers, and has fixed the attention of that dignified assembly by the singular readiness of his powers, and the maturity of his judgment. Several of the more important of his speeches have been published; as, for instance, the one delivered on the 21st of July, 1851, on the second reading of the Ecclesiastical Titles Bill; the one delivered on the second reading of the Bill for the Repeal of the Paper Duties, May 21st, 1860; and another, August 10th, 1860, on the second reading of the European Forces (India) Bill. On the formation of the Coalition Ministry of the Earl of Aberdeen, his Grace accepted a place in the Government as Lord Privy Seal (1853), which he continued to hold under the premiership of Lord Palmerston, until, in November, 1855, he exchanged it for the office of Postmaster-General. He resigned the latter appointment in 1858, and, in Lord Palmerston's Cabinet of 1859,

---

*Hogg's "Clan Campbell."

resumed his office of Lord Privy Seal, which, on the appointment of Lord Elgin to his second special mission to China in 1860, he again exchanged for the control of the Post Office. " Distinguished for the consistency of his poli-
" tical creed, the Duke of Argyll, as a foremost member of
" the Liberal Party, was called upon, on the formation of
" Mr. Gladstone's administration in December, 1868, to un-
" dertake the important post of Secretary of State for India,
" in fulfilling the duties of which he has won golden opin-
" ions as well from his own countrymen as from the people
" whom it devolves on him more immediately to govern.
" Already, in 1863, he had indicated his acquaintance with
" Indian affairs by the production of two articles, which he
" contributed severally to the January and April numbers
' of the *Edinburgh Review,* and which were afterwards sub-
" stantively published with the title of ' India under Dal-
" housie and Canning.' "

His Grace is a nobleman of varied attainments, and an earnest patron of literature, art, and science. His published works consist chiefly of addresses and lectures, a volume entitled, " The Reign of Law," and one entitled, " Iona," of which he is proprietor, and in the romantic antiquities of which he takes a deep interest.

This brief sketch of the life of His Grace the present Duke of Argyll, cannot but do injustice to a nobleman, whose active and useful life has been interwoven with most of the great public affairs of his country; but we have sought in this brief " Story of the House of Argyll," to give but a mere outline, to complete and elaborate which would require the scope of many such volumes as the present one.

THE RIGHT HONORABLE THE MARQUIS OF LORNE.

THE Right Honorable John George Edward Henry Douglas Sutherland Campbell, Marquis of Lorne, etc., present Governor-General of the Dominion of Canada, is the eldest son of His Grace the Duke of Argyll, heir to the honors and estates of the illustrious House of Campbell, and son-in-law, by marriage to H.R.H. the Princess Louise, to Her Majesty Queen Victoria. He was born at Stafford House, London, on the 6th of August, 1845, being about three years the senior of his royal wife, the birth-day of the latter being March 18th, 1848. The Marquis was early brought to the notice of Her Majesty, as will be seen from the following extract from the Queen's " Leaves from the Journal of Our Life in the Highlands, from 1848 to 1861" : " Our reception (at Inverary Castle) was in true Highland fashion ; the pipers walked before the carriage and the Highlanders on either side, as we approached the house. Outside stood the Marquis of Lorne, just two years old (August, 1847), a dear, white, fat, fair little fellow, with redish hair, but very delicate features, like both his father and mother's ; he is such a merry, independent little child. He had a black velvet dress and jacket, with a ' sporran,' scarf, and Highland bonnet."

The Marquis was educated at Eaton and Trinity College, Cambridge, and for some time commanded a company in the London Scottish Rifle Volunteers. In 1868 he was appointed private secretary to his father at the India Office; and since February of the same year he has represented the County of Argyll in the House of Commons. He resigned, of course the latter position on being appointed Governor-General of our own Dominion, to succeed Lord Dufferin.

Lord Lorne perpetuates the traditional liberalism of his family. He is a zealous supporter of the volunteer force, is a practical marksman with the rifle, and has shot with great success at the University *vs.* House of Lords and Commons matches at Wimbledon. In person, while youthful in appearance, is very handsome. He possesses an agreeable, easy manner, and an expression of great good nature and kindliness, and cannot fail to attract favourable remark from all persons of discrimination. He is possessed of considerable abilities, and although young, he has given ample evidence of both industry and capacity. As already observed, he acted for several years as private-secretary to the Duke of Argyll, his father, when Secretary of State for India, and at one time when His Grace was occupied with the preparation of an important legislative measure, Lord Lorne undertook and executed with characteristic ability, a vast amount of difficult business which seldom falls to a private secretary.

In Parliament the Marquis has distinguished himself by a conscientious independence, which led him to vote, at one time against the Gladstone ministry, of which his father was a leading member. His parliamentary career has been graceful rather than active. In every attempt to express his views he has acquitted himself in a manner becoming the great dignity of his station. Throughout he has been, like his noble father, one of the most loyal liberals.

It is recorded that Lord Lorne is considerably influenced

by the spirit of adventure, which is characterstic of his family, and of all young noblemen. This has been shown by the extent of his travels, and by the peculiar caste of his literary productions. He made his fist *début* as an author in 1867, when he published a volume of much promise, with the title of "A Trip to the Tropics, and Home through America," which is a pleasant and observant record of travel in Jamaica, Cuba, St. Domingo, and in the United States. These "Notes from Negro Lands"—as the volume is alternatively called—are extracts from letters written by the author when travelling in 1866, in January of which year he left Southampton for the West Indies. "They contain," he frankly observed, "merely superficial views of the men, manners, and things that came under my notice; but as the countries they refer to have recently been the scenes of important events, I hope they may not be without some interest." This hope, we may content ourselves with saying, is fully justified. A Canadian editor's review of the work informs us that it is really remarkable for the impartiality and clearness of the opinions expressed in it concerning the working of the republican institutions of America.

His Excellency (for we must use that title since he is now our Governor-General) has also published two volumes of poems. The one before us, "Guido and Lita : a Tale of the Riviera," appeared in 1875, and is a production of real merit. Following are the closing passages of the little volume :—

> The gallant train the church's front has gained ;
> Their Leader's steed is at the fountain reined,
> And Guido takes his Lord within to view ;
> Him whom he mourns, the sire the Paynim slew,
> Recounts the tale of those adventurous days,
> How brief its space, and yet it years outweighs !

When all is learned, the Count goes forth to stand
Upon the church's steps, and lifts his hand,
And bids his troops rank round him on the place ;
And calls for Lita, who with blushing face
Comes out to stand before him ; and he speaks ;
" Who now for glory, or for honour seeks,
Let him, from deeds done here, example take ;
Deeds of this gentle maiden, whom I make
A Lady of my land, and ask that she
Attend my court : and Guido, as for thee,
Thou too must follow ; till the realm be free
Of heathen hordes, our swords must never sleep.
Our name must be so terrible, yon deep
Shall yet refuse to bear upon its breast
The fleets it brought to startle us from rest."

Thus by his love was Guido called to brave
War on the land, war upon the wave.
By love awakened to a manly pride,
In spirit searched, and changed, and purified,
His bright renown o'er Christendom was spread,
And lived where'er the light of victory sped.

A year has passed, and where red battle burned,
Fair Peace again with blessings has returned,
And mailed processions, banished from the field,
To white-robed trains the festive town must yield.
See, to the sound of music and song,
A stately pageant slowly moves along.
Before the church's door the crowds divide ;
Hail the sweet pomp, that guards the maiden bride !
Hail the young lord, who comes this day to claim,
A prize, the guerdon of a glorious name !
They kneel before the altar, hand in hand,
While thronged around, Provence's warriors stand.
Hush ! for the sacred rites, the solemn vow,
That crowns with Faith, young Love's impetuous brow.

The prayer is said ; then, as the anthem swells
A peal rings oat of happy marriage bells ;
Grief pales and dies 'neath joy's ascending sun,
For knight, and maid, have blent their lives in one.

Some of the illustrations in the above-mentioned volume bear the characteristics of that fine art for which his royal wife has become famous.

As set forth in the previous sketch on the house of Argyll, Lord Lorne derives his title from that district of Argyllshire known as Lorne, or Lorn. The district in very ancient times was possessed by the Macdougalls, a family in those days nearly as powerful as the Macdonalds—" Lords of the Isles." From the Macdougalls it came into the royal house of the Suart, or Stewart, and the historian will remember that among the victories gained by Bruce in his eventful career was one over the Lord of Lorne in the Pass of Awe. By these changes the broad lands of Lorne passed into the hands of the Campbells of Lochow, the direct ancestors of the ducal house of Argyll ; and it has been aptly observed that they were then acquired, just as they have been recently consolidated and more firmly established than ever before, not by force of arms, but by a lucky marriage.

Although Lord Lorne is heir to all the estates of the great house of Argyll,—one of the highest in the realm, standing third in the Scottish roll of precedence among dukes,—yet we find ourselves, at this time, more directly interested in his marquisate than in his prospective dukedom. Hence, while we regret the want of space to give our readers a full description of the whole extent of Argyllshire, we may properly confine ourselves to some observations on the Land of Lorne proper. Now, the origin of this house of Lorne is surrounded with a good deal of uncertainty. Lorne is a name supposed by some to have been derived from one of those Dalriadic princes or leaders who, emigrating from the north of Ireland about A.D. 503, settled in the West Highlands, and there formed the first rude beginnings of the Scottish monarchy. These chiefs are said to have been three brothers, Fergus, Lorne and Angus, sons of Erc, a descendant of the great Celtic rulers of Ireland, and in all probability of the same or a kindred race with that which previously occupied the whole of Scotland, then called Albyn. While Fergus established himself on the southern peninsulas of Kintyre and Cowall, his brother Angus in Islay and the adjacent islands, Lorne chose the western district, thereafter known by his name. The district is on the west side of that most picturesque of Scottish lakes, Loch Awe, and for a considerable space further to the north and south. It is a region full of the deepest interest to the antiquarian. The extreme length varies from thirty to thirty-five miles, with a mean breadth of about ten. Three beautiful arms of the sea intersect it—Loch Feochan, in the south; Loch Etive, in the middle, and Loch Creran, further north. Of these the largest and most important is Loch Etive, a fine, land-locked reach of water which, in its upper half, trends away considerably to the north, while, between it and the head of Loch Awe, towers aloft, in massive strength and grandeur, Ben Cruachan, throwing his shadow, dark and broad, over the fair expanse of water at his base.* The landscape at many points of view excels in the most striking effects. In particular, the panorama that opens up to the traveller as he-

---

*McMillan's *Magazine*, 1871

comes in sight of Loch Awe from the east, is, for grandeur and beauty combined, without an equal in Great Britain. On a calm summer's day it presents a peculiarly charming picture. The eye rests on the placid waters of the lake and its beauteous islets, slumbering peacefully in the shade, their several outlines mirrored in responsive symmetry underneath; while, in the background, majestic and grand, the giant Ben, his brow, calm and unclouded, looks down his wooded slopes, as if keeping watch and ward over the lovely scene.

Turning our eyes a little more to the left, we see, stretching away to the southwest as far as the eye can reach, an irregular series of hills, embracing heath-covered and verdant flats, with many a basky dell between; here and there a neat homestead, with its herd of cattle browsing near; mayhap a shepherd half-way up the hill, directing by voice and gesture the movements of his sheep-dog, as he tends his fleecy charge. This land of Lorne is a decidedly pastoral country. Yet, behind those undulating hills, embowered in pleasant halts of green, or looking forth upon the western sea, there lie spots replete with the stirring memories of days gone by. Who would imagine that these slopes once waved with mighty forests through which rushed the fierce wild boar and scarce less savage man— that a thousand years ago this same region was the centre of active Scottish life? But our digression is too short to tell half the beauties of Lorne. It is, however, from this country that our noble Marquis derives his title, the baronial title of Lorne being, as we have before described, merged into the earldom of Argyll, thereafter becoming a courtesy title for the heir apparent of the house.

The titles of the Marquis place him among the highest

noblemen of the realm. Should he live until the death of His Grace the Duke of Argyll, his father, he will rule the noble Scottish house of Campbell, and no other house, either of Lowland or Highland origin, ever counted among its members so great and illustrious a catalogue of ennobled and otherwise distinguished individuals. In this respect the Campbells may claim superiority over the Scotts, the Hamiltons, the Murrays, the Grahams, and even the Stuarts.

Some one has used the expression that it is much for Lord Lorne that he is his father's son. We may not be able to sympathize with all the enthusiasm of the clan of Campbell; we may not all endorse the Duke of Argyll's politics, but it is impossible to hear the man, to read his books, without a feeling of respect, almost a feeling of veneration for him. Lord Lorne has done a very clever thing in making himself more famous than his famous father. He has abundant advantages. He has had the advantage of that inestimable training in politics and statesmanship which the House of Commons confers upon a youthful member, and be will come to this country well qualified, in many respects, to discharge the duties of the most important political station which has just been conferred upon him.

A word should be said here respecting the arms of the Campbells of Argyll. These are quite as numerous as the gentry bearing them, and yet a family likeness runs throughout most of them. "*Follow me,*" says the Breadalbane motto, and a cadet replies, "*Sequor*" (I follow). Such are the variations most commonly indulged in. Heraldry, in fact, is a science obviously of comparatively recent origin, it being a doubtful question whether even the Normans, with whom it certainly had its source, brought it over with them on their conquest of England, or created it afterwards. The invention seems to have really resulted with an age more advanced, when chivalry became fantastic as well as warlike. Countries and kings, no doubt, were the first to use arms. As for the majority of heraldic bearings, they are plainly attempts made by the later kings-at-arms, either to mark a peculiar event in the story of the family concerned, or to pun on the family name. The "two peasants with the yokes" of the Hays, for instance, point to the old story of the battle of Luncarty, though it is now clearly understood that the origin ascribed by that tradition to the house is utterly fictitious. Then, again, the Trotters take the half-laughable emblem in their arms of a "trotting-horse," with the motto of "Slowly Onwards" (*Festina lente*); while the Justice family take a sword and scales, and the Buntings show the device of a bunting. It is plain, in short, that these, and other cases of what is called canting heraldry, are generally the products of heralds in times later than those which saw the families founded. The arms of the house of Argyll may be thus described:—

ARMS. Quarterly: first and fourth, Girony of eight pieces, Or, and Sable; second and third, Argent, a Galley or Lymphad, sails furled up, for the Lordship of Lorne.
CREST. A Boar's head, coupeed, Or.
SUPPORTERS. Two Lions.
MOTTO. *Vix ea nostra voco* (I scarcely call all this my own). The Duke John seems to have conjoined this motto with that of *Ne obliviscaris* (Forget not), also used on an "Escrol" in the arms.
BADGE. Myrtle.
[Loudoun quarters with the Crawfords, and Breadalbane with the Stewarts of Lorne. All the families of the Campbell name bear the Oared Galley in their arms.]

We may here turn for a while to give our readers a glimpse of H. R. H. the Princess Louise, and to make some observations of her marriage with the Marquis.

H. R. H. PRINCESS LOUISE.

Her Royal Highness Princess Louise Caroline Alberta, is the fourth daughter of Her Majesty the Queen. She was born at Buckingham Palace on the 18th of March, 1848. She is very talented, and as accomplished as assiduous and well-directed culture can render one of such great and varied natural gifts. She has developed remarkable artistic accomplishments in the departments of drawing, painting and sculpture. Mrs. Thorneycroft has had the great honor of instructing the Princess in the Arts of modelling and sculpture, and has had the greater satisfaction of seeing the grandest results in her royal pupil. One of the finest productions, in this line, which the Princess has executed, is the bust of the Queen which was shown at the Royal Academy Exhibition of 1870. Other specimens of her work have been successfully exhibited to promote charitable objects in which she has taken a deep interest.

Her Royal Highness has also very decided literary tastes and is so assiduous a reader as to deserve the name of a student. She was for some years the closest companion of the Queen, her mother, and is greatly beloved by every member of the Royal family, while her great sweetness of disposition endears her to everyone within the sphere of her influence. A graceful act of appreciative kindness was performed by the Princess, in connection with her possession as one of the Lady Patronesses of the National Society for the aid of the sick and wounded. During the Franco-German war, to each of the surgeons proceeding under the auspices of the society to the hospitals of France and Belgium, she presented, in some instances personally, a handsome pocket case ornamented with her monogram and escutcheon, containing the instruments required for military surgery. On several prominent occasions of state ceremony, the Princess Louise has officiated for the Queen, and has always called forth the most enthusiastic admiration of her dignity and graciousness.

There is not a magazine, periodical or journal published in the English language which has not from time to time, during the past ten years, spoken the highest praises of Her Royal Highness, and extolled her grace and beauty. To say that she is beloved, tenderly, devotedly, by every loyal heart in the vast empire over which her gracious mother rules, is but faintly expressing the place which she has won by her noble deeds of charity, her devotion to art and literature and her sweet disposition. We make a single extract from an English magazine which may be regarded as a representative of a thousand equally expressive of appreciation of the Princess, which we might quote from as many writers did our space permit:—

"I remember so well the day when I first saw her Royal Highness the Princess Louise. It was a day in the early spring, soft and brilliant, not without showers, yet crowned with sunshine. I had made a journey of some little trouble to go to the royal Isle of Wight, for the foundation-stone was to be laid of a building belonging to an institution that was dear to me, and the Princess Louise was to lay the first stone. She has taken her part since in much more brilliant and crowded ceremonials, but I cannot but think her Royal Highness will long remember that day in the Undercliff.

I am sure that there were many there who will long remember *her*. We waited some time for the sound of her horses' hoofs, for she had to traverse the whole breadth of the island on her errand of mercy. There was a throng of fair ladies present, but as the eye wandered over that living parterre there was no more sweet and intellectual face than that of the young Princess. Her duties were long and must have been fatiguing, but they were done gracefully and well. There was one murmur of praise and congratulation. All of us remembered that day, and will always recollect it with pleasure. One slight incident occurred, but to me, a man of a loyal nature, the incident was in no wise slight. The Princess went off, *magna comitante caterva*, to a distant part of the grounds, to plant a memorial tree. I admired the courage that I dared not imitate, for the wet grass was associated in my mind with the aliments of the poor people for whom our good work was intended. But as, with a lady on my arm, I lingered by one of the pathways, it so happened that the Princess suddenly came back that way, and passed close by. We stood quite alone, and made respectively curtsey and bow, and the Princess gave us a gracious salutation and a courteous glance of her candid eyes. It was but a trifle, yet one which we valued and treasured.

We know but little of the young life of the Princess, and yet we know that it presents a fresh fair picture that might easily be shadowed forth. Happy is the nation that has no history, and happy are the princes who in contemporary history are unknown. Yet in the 'fierce light which beats upon a throne' much of the private life of the English royal family has been unveiled. The Queen herself has given us glimpses of her home and her family life. We have all been privileged to see how the fair children of Osborne and Balmoral grew up under the plastic care of the Prince Consort, and to observe evidences of the care, forethought, and tenderness with which the training and education of his children were attended. And whispers came respecting the Princess Louise on how rich a soil these fruitful germs were implanted. We were told of the rare culture and intelligence which she possessed. We see with loyal appreciation the wisdom and love which the Queen manifested towards her children. We recollect how in her Highland book there is a simple mention of her Majesty teaching her eldest child her lessons while on one of her excursions. The Queen herself has touchingly shown how she values the peace and security which a happy marriage can impart, and how little she desires for her children a position of solitary splendour like her own. In a memorandum contributed to 'The Early Years of the Prince Consort,' she says: 'A worse school for a young girl, or one more detrimental to all natural feelings and affections, cannot well be imagined, than the position of Queen at eighteen, without experience and without a husband to guide and support her. This the Queen can state from painful experience, and she thanks God that none of her dear daughters are exposed to such danger.'

We have all some knowledge of the great accomplishments of the Princess. We need hardly say that she is an accomplished artist. In the Old Bond Street Gallery of the British Institution she exhibited some works at an exhibition on behalf of the destitute widows and orphans of Germans killed in the war. 'The battle is decided; the defeated and the pursuers have passed from view before the day has quite closed in night, leaving the dead and wounded far behind. Pallid light still lingers in the deep blue sky, contrasting with the glare of a burning village; the dead and wounded, both French and German, are on the plain, and there are dismounted cannon. A sister is supporting a wounded soldier, stanching the blood, and another sister is bearing her help. It is a gleam of mercy on the battle plain.' We believe that the Princess Louise has given much practical attention to such deeds of mercy. In the Royal Academy two years ago she exhibited a bust of her royal mother, not indeed the work of a great artist, but infinitely above the ordinary level of amateurs."

When the intended marriage of Her Royal Highness with a subject of the Crown was announced, a wave of interest spread throughout the length and breadth of the nation, and the Princess became more than ever a subject of universal regard. Her acts and movements were noted with that minuteness which had previously characterized only the reports of the Queen's own doings. As evidence of this we need only present the following extract from the London *Graphic* of March 4th, 1871:—

"We were informed that before the Royal cortege entered the House of Lords on the day of the opening of Parliament, the throne presented a very inartistic appearance. The robes of state were thrown over it in such a manner as to hide the crimson velvet and display only the ermine, so that the effect was exactly as if a huge white cloth had been wrapped about a high-backed empty chair with an imitation gilt crown on the top of it. In fact it suggested reminiscences of a hair dresser's saloon. But when Her Majesty entered and seated herself, the Princess Louise with genuine artistic instinct, stooped and lifted a corner of the robes so as to display the warmer tints of the crimson velvet. Probably the act was almost involuntary on the part of the fair daughter of royalty. While her hands were thus busily occupied her thoughts were devoted to more important matters. Of what was she thinking? May we venture to guess? To some extent we may suppose that her meditations were of a somewhat solemn and chastened character. There is always something saddening in the reflection that we are doing a thing for the last time, and the Princess may have felt that in all probability she was for the last time performing her part as maiden daughter of the Queen in one of the most impressive ceremonials of English court life. Mingled with these feelings other ideas of a livelier character may have presented themselves. The grand state ceremonial then being enacted may have suggested visions of another ceremonial shortly to take place at Windsor in which the Princess, instead of playing a subordinate part, would assume the chief *rôle*."

Thus the people were not only eager to make her every

act a subject of interesting gossip, but undertook to divine her very thoughts. Indeed it must have been truly gratifying to the noble heart of the Princess, that such an intelligent people paid her such loyal homage.

It may properly constitute a part of our brief sketch of the Princess to speak of the royal wedding at Windsor Castle, when her fortunes were united with those of the house of Argyll. This took place on the 21st March, 1871, and was the chief event for a considerable period of time in Great Britain. The marriage was celebrated at St. George's chapel. The scenes outside the castle before and after the marriage merits a brief description. In short Windsor presented a gay aspect during the whole day. Soon after day-break a great number of workmen were astir, setting up loyal mottoes, complicated monograms, and extensive illuminations over the public buildings, most of the private houses in the neighbourhood the castle and the railway station. Thus when the early London trains arrived the town was already gaily bedecked with flags, banners and garlands. The morning was bleak, cold and misty, and the weather at one time seemed inclined to be somewhat unpropitious and March like. At nine o'clock a large body of police arrived from London, the sun broke through the clouds, and an hour later crowds of people anxious to secure a good view of the procession, suddenly appeared and thronged up the Castle Hill as far as the gates, where they were halted by a large police force, and allowed to enter only by ticket. Those not fortunate enough to possess the required pass stationed themselves outside the gates on each side the hill. Inside the gates were nine hundred Eton boys who had come out for the occasion, and who had been placed in files on each side of the road to welcome the bride as she drove past from her abode in the castle to the chapel.

The Castle green presented an especially lively appearance, and the troops drawn up before the chapel, and the varied toilettes of the lady spectators formed at once a gay and picturesque scene. This was still further heightened by the advent of a Highland regiment, which marched in with its bagpipes playing the appropriate air of "The Campbells are Coming"—an air to which the Grenadier Guards had marched up to the Castle Hill a few moments before. The arrival of these regiments gave great satisfaction to the crowd outside, which had become uneasy of waiting. By-and-by the royal carriages went down to the station to meet the distinguished guests of the wedding. It was not long before the procession made its appearance, and as the royal carriages rolled past a cheer was raised and hats were taken off and handkerchiefs waved as the occupants were severally recognized. The Prince and Princess of Wales seemed especially popular, and the Princess Teck was bowed to and waved at from all sides. The bridegroom was also heartily greeted, but when Her Majesty passed with the Princess Louise the cheers became universal, especially on the part of the Eton College boys, whose loyalty was enthusiastically displayed. When the procession had passed, the crowd showed no signs of dispersing, and waited patiently for the return of the royal party after the ceremony. At a quarter-past one the bells rang out a merry peal, and escorted by a guard of honor the newly wedded couple appeared, in the wedding carriage, stopping every now and then to bow to the crowd, to which the crowd, highly complimented and pleased, replied by renewed cheers. They were not lessened when the Queen and Prince of Wales, this time in the same carriage, passed by.

We must now give a few brief details of the ceremony itself. The bright sun had given a beautiful hue to the spectacle inside the chapel, and streaming through the rich colored glass, lent a warmth to what, in the nave, would otherwise have borne a cold and bare aspect. This was the portion set apart for what we may call the outside public, and the issue of tickets being limited, there was no crowding. The passage down the nave was lined on each side by ladies; behind them were the gentlemen and the yeomen of the guard in their quaint costumes; but beyond the organ-gallery stretched the choir. Gradually, as the guests dropped in, the gorgeous spectacle unfolded itself; bit of color was added to bit of color, as in the evolutions of a transformation scene. The knights' stalls, with their banners overhead, were filled with bright uniforms and dresses; there were ministers, stiff with embroidery, officials in blue and gold, and officials in red and gold, ladies in all hues and blazing with jewels; military uniforms, diplomatic uniforms, gold laced robes, silver sticks and gold sticks, and the heralds in mediaeval bibs of gold embroidery and colour. As the seats in this part of the chapel were reserved, there was much more regularity noticeable in the influx of their occupants. Those who were to take part in the ceremony arranged themselves about the altar.

The bridegroom, not in Highland costume, but in a dark Hussar uniform, and accompanied by his best men, Lord Ronald Leveson-Gower and the Earl Percy, had arrived and taken his stand in the bridegroom's place, the others being arranged in the following order:—The Princess of Wales and her children; the Count de Flandre, in Belgian uniform; the Princess Christian, in cerise satin; the Princess Beatrice, in pink; the Duchess of Cambridge; Prince Arthur, in Rifle uniform; Prince Leopold, in Highland dress; the Duke of Cambridge, in Field Marshall's uniform; Prince Christian, in uniform; the Princess Mary of Teck, and the Prince of Teck, in an Austrian Hussar uniform; the members of the bridegroom's family, including the Countess Percy and the Maharajah Dhuleep Singh and the Maharanee, the two latter in rich uniforms of gold and yellow satin; the Prince of Wales, in Hussar uniform, and the Duke of Saxe-Coburg, in a white tunic, waited by the door when the Queen and Princess would enter.

The organ now burst forth in triumphal strains as the eight bridesmaids, the heralds of the bride, made their appearance. Then there was an "alarm of trumpets," a roll of drums, and Her Royal Highness, the Princess Louise and Her Majesty the Queen entered. The bridal procession passed slowly to the altar, the Queen, who appeared in excellent spirits, bowing her acknowledgements. As the bride and her royal mother ascended the *haut-pas* the Marquis of Lorne bowed profoundly, and the wedding service began, the prelates present being the Bishops of London, Winchester, Oxford and Worcester, who were assisted by some lesser dignitaries of the church. The Bishop of London read the service, the Bishop of Winchester the epistle and exhortation; the responsive "I wills" were clearly audible, and the Marquis of Lorne and the Princess Louise were man and wife.

When the blessing had been uttered, the Queen extended her hand to her new son-in-law, who bowed and kissed it, and then with the Princess upon his arm, and followed by Her Majesty proceeded down the long passage of the choir and nave and the royal ceremony was at an end. The company subsequently assembled in the white drawing-room, where presently Her Majesty and the bride and bridegroom appeared, and made the tour of the room. The royal family and that of the Duke of Argyll then retired to luncheon. The rest of the party retired to Waterloo Gallery, where the general banquet had been laid. Shortly after four o'clock the bride and bridegroom left the castle in a carriage with two pairs of greys, accompanied by an escort of Life Guards and a shower of white satin slippers.

Such is a brief, very brief, sketch of the wedding of the Princess. The affair attracted the greater attention since it was the marriage of a daughter of the Sovereign to a subject—an event, though unusual, yet by no means without many precedents. To those, however, who could call to mind the history of such marriages in the distant past, it was a matter of great congratulation that Britain had reached an age of peace and of firm succession, when it was no longer dangerous for a princess to marry a subject who loves her. In the old times, when an Earl or Duke coveted the daughter of his king, it was often seriously discussed in Council whether such a marriage was safe for the throne. To the wealthy and powerful lord of a dozen frontier castles with the possibility of a traitorous alliance with Scottish monarchs and Welsh chieftains, it was unsafe to trust a princess, a union with whom might produce fresh claimants to the succession. Hence it is that we find the usurpers men the most ready to barter their pride and ally their daughters to powerful subjects, whose men-at-arms and archers might be useful in the rough wrangles for the crown. And hence it arose that Scotch, French, or German princes were always more in demand than the wisest, bravest and handsomest of the English nobles, because their alliances were useful in foreign entanglements into which our kings so often fell. A Breton prince had ports into which war vessels could put and discharge their cargoes of bowmen and swordsmen that were to ravage the pastures of Champagne and the vineyards of Burgundy; a princess bestowed on a Scotchman saved the English borders from ceaseless forrays; but it was only at special seasons that an Earl of Pembroke or an Earl of Leicester could win a lady of royal birth. These hard times have gone now. Barons no longer defy the crown in Yorkshire, and Cheshire cannot be roused into rebellion; nor are love's claims any longer to be frowned down by grave councillors, and pretenders to the throne are never countenanced.

But let us digress, if indeed digression it be, to look at some of the English princesses who have married subjects. The first was Eleanor, the third daughter of the cruel usurper John. At the age of five she was betrothed to the eldest son of the Earl of Pembroke, the conqueror of Ireland, who had established Henry III. upon the throne. The English nobles, jealous at the match, postponed the marriage for a long time, urging that a king's daughter should be married to a powerful foreign ally of England, and ought not to be thrown away on a mere subject. But the friends of Pembroke contending that the Earl was powerful both in Wales and Ireland, brought forward precedents of princesses of France having married subjects, and the marriage at last took place. The Earl was more than forty and only survived the marriage two years, during which time he and his young wife of fifteen lived together with much affection. Eleanor afterwards secretly married Simon de Montfort, the son of the persecutor of the Albigenses, in violation of an oath she had taken on her first widowhood, that she would never again become a wife.

Isabella, the eldest daughter of Edward III. married a French nobleman, the young Lord de Coucy, a French hostage sent over to England after Poictiers. He remained a firm friend to England during nearly all the disastrous French war, and it is recorded, that " Never did the English hurt man or woman or take a farthing from them who said, ' I belong to the Lord de Coucy.' " Eventually, Coucy, unable to remain any longer neutral, joined the cause of his country and sent his royal wife back to England.

Cecilia, third daughter of Edward IV., was bethrothed before she was twenty to James, the son of James III. of Scotland, but the match was broken off. After this she passed a troublesome career for some years, till Henry VII. became king, after which her life was tranquil and happy. Cecilia bore her nephew, Prince Arthur to the front, but he never reached the throne, and at the coronation of her sister Elizabeth she occupied a place of honour. At this latter ceremony was present John, Lord Wells, half-uncle to the king and the princess's future husband. This nobleman had shared in the Duke of Buckingham's unsuccessful revolt and had then fled and joined his exiled nephew at the Breton Court. It is said that Henry VII. kept Cecilia in the background, not wishing his wife's sister to marry, as in case of his own wife's failing in issue, Cecilia would be rightful heiress to the crown. The marriage was, therefore, probably clandestine, but it was a happy union, though the gentleman was twice the age of the lady. Her husband died in 1498, but the young widow did not mourn long, for she was a train-bearer among the bridesmaids of Catherine of Arragon, only three years after her husband's death.

Later she married one Thomas Kymbe, an obscure Lincolnshire person, of whom nothing is known. She had two children by her second marriage, became rather poor, and died four years after her marriage and was buried in the Abbey of Quarrera in the Isle of Wight.

Annie, the fifth daughter of Edward IV. was solicited in marriage before she was four years old, by Maximillian Duke of Austria, for his young son Phillip. The bride's portion was to be 100,000 crowns, but the match fell through. The Countess eventually married Lord Thomas Howard, the son of the Earl of Surry, whom Henry VII. committed for a time to the Tower. The king, who was far too fond of money, did not bestow on the Princess Anne the bridal portion of 10,000 marks bequeathed to her by her father, and the king's displeasure and fines prevented the Earl of Surry making any great provision for the young couple. Annie did not appear much at Court, and died early in life. She was buried in Thetford Priory.

Catherine, the next daughter of Edward IV., married a Courtenay, a member of a family which boasted French kings and Greek Emperors among its ancestry. The young Earl Courtenay seems to have been a nobleman of great virtue and skilled in all chivalrous accomplishments. The princess and her husband lived in great splendor down in Devonshire, and Courtenay distinguished himself by defending Exeter against Perkin Warbeck and his brother rebels. Her son was executed by Henry VIII. for daring to correspond with his relative, the celebrated Cardinal Pole.

Mary Tudor, third daughter of Henry VII. was the most beautiful and accomplished princess of her time. Erasmus saw her sporting about the royal nurseries at Eltham and made a note of the fact. She was educated in all the accomplishments of her time, learnt French and Latin, played upon the lute, clavichord, and regals and danced with more than usual grace. An early treaty of marriage with the Prince of Castle was broken off before the accession of Henry VIII. Mary then fell in love with Sir Charles Brandon, one of the bravest soldiers and most refined courtiers of his age. Brandon was the son of Henry VIII.'s standard bearer at the battle of Bosworth, and had been chosen by Prince Henry, afterwards Henry VIII., as one of his familiar attendants. Having been twice married he fell in love with the Princess Mary, who was at that very time being wooed by Louis XII. of France, an old king fast hastening to his death. Mary consented to the match on the express condition that if she survived her husband she should not be constrained but permitted to marry wherever she pleased. The delighted old man showed the Earl of Worcester, the English ambassador, who concluded the marriage contract, a huge chest burning with jewels, for one of which 100,000 ducats had been refused. "These are for my wife," said the old king, "but she shall not have them at all at once, for I must have divers kisses and thanks for them." "I assure you," wrote the Earl of Wolsey, "he thinketh every hour of the day till he seeth her; he is never well, never until he heareth speaking of her." The doting old monarch wrote with his own hand to Wolsey, "Make my compliments to my good brother the king, your master, and tell him that I beg him to send his sister as soon as possible, and that in doing so he will be conferring on me a great pleasure." Mary by no means so eager to meet her bridegroom took with her six Italian dresses and eight English, besides such store of plate and jewels that

Louis generously forgave 200,000 crowns of the dowery. Her reception by the old king was of a magnificent description; what with bouquets, pageants, jousts, and the grand coronation ceremony when the chivalrous Francis of Valois stood behind the young Queen and held the crown above her head, so that its weight might not oppress her. The Duke of Suffolk (Charles Brandon) was one of King Henry's ambassadors on this occasion, and distinguished himself greatly at the jousts. There seems, indeed, to have been a mutual jealously between the French and English knights, and Suffolk must, moreover, have been in a reckless kind of humor and ready to do anything to prove his valor before the lady of his love. He dealt about him so desperately, wounding one French knight unto death, that Francis, who had himself been wounded, is said to have hired a gigantic German to go in and do battle with the Englishman. But Suffolk's blood was up and the big German was overthrown. Leigh Hunt says that Brandon carried the German shield as a trophy to the young Queen who, in the course of the jousting, had cried out, "Hurt not my sweet Charles," but these particulars belong to the world of legend rather than to that of history. We only know that Suffolk bore himself gallantly in the lists, being one of the strongest of English knights, and we may suppose that Mary admired him none the less for beating her new countryman. The old king did not long survive the marriage, and in a short time the royal widow retired to the Hotel de Clugny to spend in bed the usual six weeks mourning insisted on by French etiquette. Now follows the contest. Princes and emperors and kings bring their power and influence against the suit of Charles, but in spite of kings and emperors and princes, true love prevails and the secret marriage took place in the little oratory chapel of the Hotel de Clugny, only ten persons, including the French king, being present. Brandon immediately broke matters to Wolsey, who could smoothe everything. "My Lord of York," he wrote abjectly, "when I came to Paris I learned many things which put me in great fear and so did the Queen both, and the *Queen would never let me have no rest*" (this was rather shabby of Brandon, and, above all, decidedly bad grammar), " till I had granted her to be married, and so, to be plain with you, *I have married her heartily.*" This nearly cost Brandon his life. Long afterwards, when Brandon and Wolsey quarrelled about the king's divorce, Wolsey said reproachfully to Brandon : " Sir, of all men within this realm, you have least cause to be offended with Cardinals, for if I, a simple Cardinal had not been, you should have had at this present no head upon your shoulders."

Great altercation ensued between the two Courts as to the jewels, etc., which Mary was to take back to England. Over these treasures Francis and Henry wrangled like two Jew salesmen. Eventually, Mary pining for England, received half the jewels and 30,000 crowns for her expenses. Her marriage was celebrated in Greenwich, and all went well. The portraits of the Duke and Duchess were painted and underneath appeared the lines, probably written by Suffolk himself :—

> Cloth of gold, do not despise,
> Though thou be matched with cloth of frize ;
> Cloth of frize, be not too bold,
> Though thou be matched with cloth of gold.

The beautiful Mary died in 1533. Within a short time the Duke married again, a beautiful girl of fourteen. Mary was the last princess who openly married a subject, but in two other instances princesses are supposed to have allied themselves to persons below them in rank. Elizabeth, eldest daughter of James I., who married the Prince Palatine, the unfortunate King of Bohemia, died soon after her return to England, leaving her jewels to Prince Rupert and her papers and portait to Lord Craven—a brave, chivalrous old officer, to whom many supposed her to have been secretly married. Mary, the eldest daughter of Charles I., who married the Prince of Orange, also ended her days in England. The rumor that she secretly married Harry Jennyn, a young nobleman of Charles II.'s Court, was, perhaps after all, without foundation.

A word in this connection concerning the Marriage Act will be of interest. The Royal Marriage Act was enacted in 1792 in consequence of the secret marriage of the Duke of Glocester with Maria, the Countess Dowager of Waldegrave. The private marriage of the Duke of Cumberland in 1771 with Lady Ann Luttrell, widow of Mr. Christopher Boston, of Derbyshire, augmented the vexation of King George, and the result was, an Act forbidding any of the royal family contracting marriage without the royal sanction while under the age of twenty-five years. After this period they were at liberty to solemnize the proposed union, even if the royal sanction was withheld, if, after having announced their intention to the Privy Council, an entire year should elapse without either House of Parliament addressing the king against it.

In the case of the marriage of H. R. H. the Princess Louise with the Marquis of Lorne, on the 21st March, 1871, the hearts of all true and loyal subjects of the Queen were rejoiced. There were none to oppose ; nor were there any dangers to the crown to result from the union. The royal wedding we have already partially described. The royal wedding cake was greatly admired for its elegance and artistic skill. It stood upon a circular gold plateau five inches high; the height of the cake itself being five feet. The lower part was in eight compartments, two with the Princess's coat of arms and two with the Marquis's and four oval medallions with their initials arranged in a monogram. These were divided from each other by eight figures of boys on thermed scroll pedestals, connected by festoons of orange blossoms and leaves, and supporting an open arch balcony, and vases on stands containing bouquets of orange blossoms and sprigs of Scotch heather, etc. The centre represented a temple, with steps leading to the inside; the interior contained a circular shell shaped basin or stand with four doves on the edge drinking from it. The exterior had eight Corinthian pillars, and at the four angles were figures of fine art, science, agriculture, and commerce, with thistles and roses in relief on the base of the stand; over this was a second but smaller temple with eight twisted pillars and figures between them, representing the four seasons. The next was a circular stand decorated with scroll work and, the whole was surmounted with a figure of Hebe. The ornaments were molded, cast, and entirely worked in pure sugar. The cake was designed by Mr. S. Ponder, Her Majesty's Chief Confectioner, and occupied him and his assistants nearly three months in preparation and manufacture. Besides this, which was *the* wedding cake, there was another, which had been presented by the Prince and Princess of Wales and made by the Chester confectioner.

Our lady readers will eagerly scan a description of the royal wedding presents, which must be brief. We can only mention a few of the most prominent. Among those presented by Her Majesty was a handsome locket, the centre being formed by a very fine Emerald and the setting of diamonds richly encrusted. The tiara, the gift of the Duke and Duchess of Argyll, is also formed of Emeralds and diamonds, surmounted by a graceful scroll-work of the same jewels. The Marquis of Lorne's present was a beautiful pendant ornament, with a large and fine sapphire mounted with brilliants and pearls and pearl drop, the centre forming a bracelet. The loyal people of Mull presented the Princess with a bracelet, a massive ornament of gold set with Scotch pearls and richly decorated with artistic gold work in the Runic style. The present from the upper servants and tenantry of Balmoral consisted of a necklace and ear-rings. The former were composed of twenty-eight fine Scotch pearls, well matched and of rare size and orient, connected by lozenge-shaped links of gold. The pendant, designed from the antique, contained four very large Scotch pearls in a chased scroll work of gold, ending with a fine pear-shaped pearl. The earrings are formed of two large pearls, set with four brilliants in a quatrefoil, separated by a blue enamel line from the gold border, studded with small diamonds. A diamond ornament at the top and a pendant of three diamonds completes the design.

One of the most interesting tokens of affection and loyalty accepted by the Princess Louise was the Bible and casket presented by 4,755 maidens of the United Kingdom, whose subscriptions were limited from one penny to one shilling. The binding, of Morocco leather, consists of a red cross on royal purple ground, both enriched with gold; the arms of the cross embrace four sunk panels of white, adorned with the English rose and foilage in gold; in the centre is a monogram of crossed L's and a coronet enclosed in cusped quatrefoil, and a row of enriched quatrefoils, alternately red and white, fill up the space at the top and bottom. The clasps harmonize with the general design. The edges in front bear arms and coronet, amidst emblems relieved by scrolls, inscribed, " Search the Scriptures," and " Thy Word is Truth ;" on the top the Passion Flower, and on the scrolls " God is Love," and " God is Light ;" at the bottom, lillies of the valley with snowdrops, and " Be Watchful," " Be Zealous." The vellum fly leaves bear the coronet and monogram, and the inscription, " To Her Royal Highness the Princess Louise Caroline Alberta, with the loyal, loving and prayerful wishes of the maidens of her native land, March 21st, 1871." The casket is in English oak, with the sides enriched with diapered panels, and the top with carving of rose and thistle, supporting the arms and coronet emblazoned, and is beautifully executed.

Her Majesty also presented the Royal bride with a necklace of five large opals, set round with brilliants or connected by festoons of diamonds, a large drop branch with two very fine opals, set round with brilliants, and a pair of opal and diamond earrings. Among the other presents were the clan Campbell jewel, the hair-pins given by the Princes Arthur and Leopold and the Princess Beatrice and the locket given by the Dowager Duchess of Argyll. The first consists of a necklace of pearls and diamonds, from which hangs a locket of oval form, with pendant; the centre of the locket is formed by a large and extremely beautiful oriental pearl, surrounded by a closely set row of diamonds of large size, but set in such a manner as to give an appearance of lightness very seldom obtained in ornaments of a similar description; the pendant, the most characteristic portion of the jewel, is suspended by an emerald sprig of bog myrtle (the Campbell badge) and bears in the centre the gally of Lorne, composed of sapphires on a pave of diamonds; the border, also of sapphires and diamonds, bears the inscription "no obliviscaris." The hair-pins, of which there are two, are ornamented with the diamond daisy flowers. The locket has a crystal centre for hair, and is enclosed in a diamond border.

The two necklaces are the gifts respectively of the people of Kentyre and Tyree. The former consists simply of a double row of very fine large pearls fastened with a pearl snap, and, what is a rare thing in a necklace of this size, all the pearls are perfect. The other necklace is interesting, as having been made from the design of the Princess Louise herself. The balls are of a marble peculiar to the district of Tyree. A magnificent silver tankard was a present from the Eton boys to the Marquis of Lorne. It is richly chased all over with battle subjects, after Le Brun, and the handle is formed of Satyrs. On the base are two inscription plates, one bearing the arms of Eton College and the other the words, "Presented to the Marquis of Lorne on his marriage by the present members of his old school, Eton, 1871."

The lockets presented by the Princess to each of her bridesmaids, are of a novel character and were executed from the design of Her Royal Highness, an adaptation from a beautiful Holbien design of *cristal de roche*, beautifully engraved with a wreath of roses and forget-me-nots, blended and emblazoned in proper colours and having in the centre a royal purpole scroll, upon which is placed the name "Louise" in gold letters. The whole is surrounded by a border of blue and white enamel on gold tracery inlaid with pearls, and hangs from a true lover's knot of turquoise enamel surmounted by the Princess's coronet studded with emeralds and rubies.

But we must close our observations on the Royal wedding presents, having mentioned only a few of the more prominent gifts. Others, too numerous for even enumeration here, attested the loyalty of a great people, and evinced the high esteem in which Her Royal Highness was regarded by all.

The following epithalamium for Her Royal Highness the Princess Louise on the occasion of her marriage came from a loyal heart and a ready pen. If we are not mistaken it was first published in a London weekly journal.

I.

Grander than thunder-peal,
When parting clouds reveal
The sudden lightning on the summer sky;
  Grander than wildest roar
  Of billows on the shore
When ocean chafes with wrath, and clenches high
His tortuous fingers in the shrouds and masts
Of mighty ships that splinter in the blasts;
  Grander than trumpet sound
  When armies shake the ground
Returned from victory, is the people's voice,
When shouts the multitude, "Rejoice! Rejoice!"

II.

Not oft such sound is heard
  Far echoing over land and sea;
Not oft a nation's heart is stirr'd
  To such deep burst of love and loyalty,
    As on this jubilant day
    Our British Isles display

To her, serene, who steppeth down
From the cold attitudes where gleams the crown,
To take her bridegroom by the hand,
And pass with him into the happier land
To the warm valleys where the roses blow,
And the winds scatter odours as they go.

III.

Step down, fair daughter of the Isles,
In pride of glowing youth,
Arrayed in purity of maiden smiles,
And innocence and truth,
Step down, Louise, and find
Instead of icicles on lofty peaks,
The sympathetic touch of human kind,
And answering welcome upon friendly cheeks ;
Step down into the world with gladsome heart,
And love shall follow thee, where'er thou art.

IV.

When nations cheer the lustful lords of war,
   Or strew with flowers a blood-stained conqueror's path,
And joke themselves like helots to the car
   Of martial glory-deifying Wrath ;
We know their shouts are idle sound
   That they are fain to curse if apt to bless ;
That were their hero to the scaffold bound
   For the high treason of an unsuccess,
Their groans, their scorn, their hisses, and their hate,
   Would surge around his weak, defenceless head,
Till the last blow of unrelenting Fate
   Had lain him with the dead.

V.

Not such the cheers, O bonnie bride of Lorne,
That swell through Britain on thy bridal morn,

Not such the homage that from bower and town,
From field and mead and sea-surveying down,
From Scottish hill and English plain,
And Irish moorland pours like freshning rain,
On thee and thine with fervour of accord—
On thee and on thy heart's dear Lord.

Oh no ! a homage more sincere
Loads every shout and floats on every cheer,
Homage spontaneous and unsought,
Only by modest virtue bought,
Born of the people's love, and all their holiest thought.

VI.

Pass down, Louise, pass down
  Among the people, and be one of them !
Love is a noble crown,
  A more resplendent diadem
Than King or Kaiser ever won or stole.
  Thou hast it ; wear it on thy matron brow,
  Ever as bright and beautiful as now
When virgin blushes show the virgin soul !
  Happy as maiden, happier still as wife,
  May peace and joy attend thy life
And in thy home all earthly bliss abide,
Daughter of England ! Scotland's hope and pride !

It is not at all surprising that such an event should stir the poetic genius of the land. On the other hand, there was everything in the occasion to excuse even an aspirant-poet for making his first effort. But the theme was by no means confined to poetical adventurers. Skilled genius, ripened talent, and eminent scholarship enriched the verse which gave, for a brief period, a distinctitve Princess Louise characteristic to the then current English literature. There is one piece entitled, "Louise of Lorne," written over the signature of H. Savile Clarke, and published on the occasion of the royal wedding, which has been treasured by the writer for a considerable period, and which is prized alike for the event to which it refers, and for the beautiful sentiments it expresses:

LOUISE OF LORNE.

They flung the banners out to shine
    On Windsor's immemorial towers,
And gathered to Saint George's shrine
    All spring-tide blazonry of flowers.
The organ's diapason roll'd
    In thunder down the trophied aisle;
The wedding circlet, wrought of gold,
    Gave a new daughter to Argyll.

Rejoice, O Scotland, from the north
    Where those wild islets fret the tide,
To Teviotdale and foam-fleck'd Forth,
    And story-haunted Border-side.
The rose of England twined yestreen
    With heather from the mountain crest;
Love well the daughter of our Queen,
    For the brave heart within her breast.

She dared to love, and dared to mate
    As lowlier maidens love and wed,
She stoop'd from all her high estate,
    And " Love is lord of all,' she said—
" For that high hope of equal love,
    The one elixir sweetening life,
I yield me to his arms to prove,
    No Princess, but a faithful wife."

'Mid all the costly offerings laid
    Before thee, homage to express,
Thou wilt not scorn the one gift made
    By poor hearts that can only bless.

In sooth, from every heart that beats
   In Britain 'twixt the silver seas,
A benison thy bridal greets
   For all the years to come, Louise !

O noble bridegroom, guard her well,
   The brightest jewel of thy line,
For proudly shall thy children tell,
   Of all she left for thee and thine.
And may the future be as fair
   As certes was that fair March morn,
When Princes prayed the Church's prayer ;
   " God's blessing on Louise of Lorne."

THE NEW GOVERNOR-GENERAL—OPINIONS.

The arrival of Her Royal Highness Princess Louise, and her husband, the Right Honorable the Marquis of Lorne, as Governor-General of the Dominion, almost simultaneously with the late decided political reaction in Canada, gives a new interest to the affairs of the country. So much is this the case that we find Canadian affairs at once assuming a more prominent place in the columns of the leading journals in both Great Britain and the United States. In the latter, and to too great an extent in the former also, but little mention has heretofore been made of passing events in this country. The press seems to have taken it for granted that Canadian news ceased to be of any interest to the general reader when it passed beyond the Canadian boundary. American newspapers have professed the greatest good will for Canada, and yet they have never omitted to improve every good opportunity of displaying their poor wit at our expense. The English press has graciously accorded us a fifth rate position in the scale of general importance, and has always mistaken the commercial enterprise and political energy of this country for imprudence and disloyalty; but the while, we have been slowly but really progressing, marching forward, rising in the scale of wealth and influence, and increasing in the estimation of our neighbours. The appointment of the Marquis of Lorne, partly on account of the Marquis himself, but mainly because his appointment involves the residence of royalty in Canada, has given us a new attraction—one that is likely to be of great advantage. Already much has been said on both sides of the Atlantic since the appointment was announced; and it is not a little interesting to notice the general tenor of these remarks. Harper's *Weekly* (George William Curtiss) which prides itself on saying witty things about Canada and which has not altogether outgrown its native dislike of all that is British, observed that, " If "Canada's loyalty to the mother country needed strength-" ening, or if it was thought desirable to confirm the hold " of the aristocratic spirit of the Dominion, nothing could " have been better devised than the appointment of the " Marquis and the Princess. It is possible that the natural "tendencies towards the United States of an English " colony upon this continent which is virtually independent " might have been suspected, or some signs of it discovered, " and that a ministry which is nothing if not 'imperial' " might have wished to withstand them. For what would " it advantage a Jingo Administration to make the Queen " Empress of India, yet lose Canada? The signs of such " a tendency are not very obvious, and they will not be " hastened by any thing upon the side of this country but "perfect good-will. It is, however, evident that the pre- " sence of the Queen's daughter in Canada will invest the " country with new interest to the Great Republic, which, " as the London *Times* intimates, if it chooses to spell itself " with a great R, is quite willing to spell Queen with a " great Q."

It is quite satisfactory to Canadian pride that a journal which is so reluctant in its admissions of our loyalty to the Crown, finds that *the signs of our tendencies towards the*

United States are not very obvious. And we have still greater satisfaction in informing the *Weekly* that if any such *tendencies* ever existed, and we are not willing to admit that they have to any great extent, they are forever hereafter to be a thing of the past. It is true, however, that the presence of Her Royal Highness in the Dominion will strengthen the great loyalty of the Canadian people to the Crown and kingdom of Great Britain, and may we not also add, since the *Weekly* has placed this event by the side of the political reaction in Canada, that this National Policy, which is so objectionable to Americans, may tend to the same glorious end. If we properly understand it, and if the policy is loyally carried out, we predict for it this result, and still more—that of comparative commercial independence. The latter is not earnestly desired by our Yankee friends.

The news that Her Royal Highness and the Marquis of Lorne were coming to Canada, the latter as Governor-General, was received by Canadians of every political faith with the greatest favor and approbation. The Toronto *Globe*, edited by the Honorable Senator George Brown, which expresses the sentiments of the great Liberal party of Canada, gave utterance to words of approval of the appointment in the most loyal terms. The article is worthy of preservation :—" The appointment of the Marquis of Lorne
" to the Governorship of Canada is one of the surprises in
" which the venerable Prime Minister of England delights.
" We doubt whether any administrator less enterprising
" would have conceived the idea of sending the son-in-law of
" the Queen to this country. As a matter of course Lord
" Lorne's appointment will be received in Canada with
" universal joy. Her Majesty and her councillors have

" displayed the utmost good will towards the Dominion in
" the choice they have made. No selection could have
" shown greater confidence in the future of this country,
" and none could be more beneficial. It will turn all eyes
" in Britain towards Canada, it will bring thousands of
" tourists to admire our natural scenery and study our
" material resources, and will secure for us even a greater
" share than otherwise we would have had of the great
" emigration which must necessarily take place when active
" prosperity is again made manifest on this continent. We
" are sure that every inhabitant of Canada, of whatever
" origin, will receive with gratitude this latest exhibition
" by the Queen of the kindly good-will which she has always
" shown toward the Dominion.

" The Marquis of Lorne and his consort will receive a
" loyal welcome in Canada, and nothing will be spared to
" render their residence agreeable. As a matter of course,
" the change of position will be, for them, a trying one.
" We have few attractions for the rich and great in this
" country. Those who find enjoyment in the show and
" glitter of life are not apt to think well of Canada. It so
" happens, however, that both the Marquis of Lorne and his
" consort are possessed of qualities which render them in-
" dependent of many sources of amusement. The Marquis
" is of literary tastes, with a disposition to engage in public
" business. He comes of a race which for many generations
" has earned distinction in the service of the State, and is
" not likely to feel *ennuye* in the responsible post which he is
" about to assume. The Princess has artistic tastes which
" can be indulged almost as well at Ottawa as at London,
" and like all the daughters of the Queen, she is clever and
" industrious. It remains to be seen whether this intelli-

"gent pair can find in Canada sufficient of interest to induce them to remain during the duration of a Governor-General's term. It has been said, we know not with what truth, that the Marquis of Lorne's position in England is an anomalous one, and not always agreeable. We sincerely trust that he will find in Canada a career suited to his tastes and talents.

"The Canadian people are by no means wealthy, and there will be cause for regret if the presence of the Marquis and his wife is the signal for the introduction of extravagance in equipage or dress. Apprehensions upon this score may, we hope, be laid aside. The Queen has always shown a proper sense of economy in the management of her family, and we have no doubt that her daughter and son-in-law will exhibit to the people of Canada the useful example of a prudently regulated household.

"The Marquis will unquestionably prove an excellent constitutional ruler, and the presence of the daughter of the Queen will bring joy to the hearts of thousands of loyal Canadians. The arrangement may not be permanent, the experiment may never be repeated, but no harm seems likely to arise from the appointment."

The Montreal *Gazette*, the leading Liberal-Conservative journal of the Dominion, edited by Thos. White, Esq., M.P., approved of Lord Lorne's appointment in the following terse and unmistakable language: — " In choosing a successor for Lord Dufferin, Lord Beaconsfield had no easy task. But he has performed the task in a manner which at once shows his high regard for Canada and is a merited compliment to Lord Dufferin. Although the Marquis of Lorne is as yet a young man, having been born in 1845,

" he has already done something more than give promise
" of a successful career. He has had, in consideration of
" his age, a pretty long parliamentary experience, and has
" shown himself to possess those qualities of which states-
" men are made. He is a scholar and an author, like his
" predecessor. Socially, he occupies one of the most ex-
" alted positions in the Empire. But what should make
" his appointment especially grateful to Canada, is his
" affinity to our Gracious Sovereign. As the husband of
" the Princess Louise, he is included within the sacred circle
" of royalty itself. With the Queen's daughter at our
" Capital, we certainly cannot complain that a low value is
" set upon Canada's loyalty, either by the Government or
" the Throne. If such an honour has any precedent in the
" colonial history of Great Britain, it is certainly rare, and
" we have reason to be glad that Canada has been, of all the
" foreign possessions of the Crown, singled out for so great
" a distinction. There was, indeed a rumor, some time ago,
" that one of the Princes, the Duke of Connaught, might
" be our next Governor-General. Those who can recall his
" sojourn amongst us in 1869 and 1870 would, no doubt, have
" been gratified if such an appointment had been made.
" But it would be both disloyal and unchivalrous if we were
" now to regret the passing over of that alternative. With
" a Princess as chief lady of the Dominion, her royal mother
" will be as fully represented as by a Prince. And, by all
" accounts, Her Royal Highness is, apart from considera-
" tions of rank, just the one that we should choose for the
" vacant position. Accomplished, intellectual, and amiable
" —with such a leader in our vice-regal court, Canada can-
" not fail to be benefitted socially and every way. Yet,
" notwithstanding all the advantages with which he comes,

THE GOVERNOR-GENERAL. 117

" the Marquis of Lorne will have to be endowed with no
" ordinary qualities, if he succeeds in winning amongst us
" the high reputation of Lord Dufferin. It will be long,
" very long, before his memory and that of the gentle lady
" who with him shares our affection and esteem, can be
" effaced from the minds of our population. And gladly as
" we shall be prepared to welcome to the highest station in
" our land the noble Marquis of Lorne and the daughter of
" our Queen, there will still be mingled with that welcome
" a feeling of regret for those whom a whole nation delighted
" to honour."

The English papers were also outspoken in approval of
the appointment. The following, taken from the *Graphic*,
fairly represents the spirit of them all: "It is a long time
" since any public appointment has been so well received as
" that of Lord Lorne to be Governor-General of Canada.
" He himself is believed to have some qualities which
" eminently fit him for the post, but it is the presence of
" his wife at Ottawa which will give its special character to
" his term of office. There used to be a prevailing impres-
" sion that England did not much care about her colonies,
" and would be heartily glad when she could get rid of the
" burden they impose upon her. The present Government
" has made it one of the main objects of its policy to combat
" this notion, and it could not have hit upon a happier de-
" vice than that of sending out a daughter of the Queen to
" the very colony which, in the event of a war with the
" United States, it would be most difficult to defend. She
" will probably be all the more popular because of the Re-
" publican institutions across the border, and will help the
" Canadians to realize more vividly than ever their relation
" not only to England but to the whole Empire of which

"England is the centre. It is to be hoped that the Government will be able to give fresh applications to the idea it has so happily struck out. Why should not the Duke of Connaught represent the Queen in Ireland? And might it not be possible to make Prince Leopold Viceroy of India? If the members of the Royal Family were employed in this way, a certain lustre would be shed on the great offices at the disposal of the Crown, and a good answer would be provided to ill-natured questions as to the uses of princes."

But it is important to notice that the appointment of the Marquis to be our Governor-General received the warmest approval of Lord Dufferin previous to his retirement from the post. His Excellency's speech in reply to the address of the municipal corporations of Ontario was mainly devoted to his successor, the Marquis, and his royal wife the Princess Louise. No Governor could be more warmly introduced to the people over whom he was to be placed. "It has been my good fortune to be connected all my life long with his family," said Lord DUFFERIN, "by ties of the closest personal friendship. Himself I have known, I may say, almost from his boyhood, and a more conscientious, high-minded, or better qualified Viceroy could not have been selected......His public school and college education, his experience of the House of Commons, his large personal acquaintance with the representatives of all that is most distinguished in the intellectual world of the United States, his literary and artistic tastes, his foreign travel, will all combine to render him intelligently sympathetic with every phase and aspect of your national life." His "good Whig stock" was not forgotten; and Lord DUFFERIN was very sure that a man whose ancestors had given

two martyrs to religious and political freedom would not, as the representative of the crown, encroach on the privileges of Parliament or the independence of the people. In a still higher strain he praised the Princess LOUISE; and then, with excellent humor, he said: " Lord LORNE has, as
" I have said, a multitude of merits; but even spots will be
" discovered on the sun, and unfortunately an irreparable
" and, as I may call it, a congenital defect attaches to this
" appointment. Lord LORNE is not an Irishman. [Great
" laughter.] It is not his fault—he did the best he could
" for himself. [Renewed laughter.] He came as near the
" right thing as possible by being born a Celtic Highlander.
" [Continued laughter.] There is no doubt the world is
" best administered by Irishmen. [Hear, hear.] Things
" never went better with us either at home or abroad than
" when Lord PALMERSBON ruled Great Britain [cheers],
" Lord MAYO governed India [cheers], Lord MONCK direct-
" ed the destinies of Canada [cheers], and the ROBINSONS,
" the KENNEDYS, the LAFFANS, the CALLAGHANS, the GORES,
" the HENNESSEYS, administered the affairs of our Austra-
" lian colonies and West India possessions. [Applause.]
" Have not even the French at last made the same discovery
" in the person of Marshal M'MAHON? [Laughter and ap-
" plause.] But still we must be generous, and it is right
" Scotchmen should have a turn. [Laughter.] After all,
" Scotland only got her name because she was conquered by
" the Irish (great laughter), and if the real truth were
" known, it is probable the house of Inverary owes most of
" its glory to its Irish origin. [Applause.] Nay, I will go
" a step further—I would even let the poor Englishman
" take an occasional turn at the helm [great laughter], if
" for no better reason than to make him aware how much

"better we manage the business. [Renewed laughter.] "But you have not come to that yet, and though you have "been a little spoiled by having been given three Irish "Governor-Generals in succession, I am sure that you will "find your new Viceroy's personal and acquired qualifica-"tions will more than counterbalance his ethnological dis-"advantages."

The comments of the London (Eng.) *Times* have more than an ordinary significance since they deal not only with the fitness of the Marquis for the post, but enter upon Canadian affairs generally : "We publish with great pleasure the "announcement that the Marquis of Lorne has accepted "the office of Governor-General of the Dominion of Canada, "and will enter upon his duties in immediate succession to "Lord Dufferin. The announcement will be hailed with "enthusiasm by Canadians and in this country, will be re-"garded with the greatest satisfaction. The Ministry were "apparently placed in a position of embarrassment by the "fact that Lord Dufferin's term of office which the wise and "wholesome rule of Colonial Service limits to six years ex-"pired a few weeks ago. It was felt difficult to select "any successor to Earl Dufferin who would not find his "reputation overshadowed by the memory of the most "popular of governors. There was, however, one kind of "selection which was at once impressive and likely to pro-"duce substantial political advantages, a direct connection "between the throne and the representative of the Queen's "authority in Canada is certain to be welcomed by the "colonists warmly, because their loyalty has of late been "stirred by the eloquent appeals of the retiring Governor-"General. The choice of the husband of one of Her Majes-"ty's daughters to represent the sovereignty of the Queen

"in Canada will appeal to the sentiments and traditions of
"imperial unity and the historic pride which have recently
"acquired fresh life and vigour. It is very satisfactory to
"learn that the Marquis of Lorne has not declined the re-
"sponsibility involved in the succession to Lord Dufferin.
"The services in his power, and not less in that of the
"Princess Louise, to render the Empire are great. The
"opportunity of rendering them is worth purchasing at the
"cost of some inconvenience. Never was there a better
"chance for completing a consolidating work which has
"been well begun. The feelings of Canadians towards the
"Mother country a few years ago were curiously mingled,
"their attachment to 'Home,' which is one of the striking
"characteristics of Englishmen and their descendants in
"newly settled countries was crossed with irritation at
"what they considered the coldness and neglect, social and
"political, of which they had to complain, being convinced
"that the dominant party in the Imperial Parliament were
"longing and searching for an excuse to get rid of them,
"they bitterly resented this, but, unfortunately, the game
"of cross purposes, in which several Colonial Secretaries
"took part, prevented the colonists from showing a certain
"hostile school of politicians at home that they were
"wrong. Those politicians contended that the Colonists
"wished to do nothing for themselves, but throw every re-
"sponsibility and every expense upon the Mother Country.
"When that period of vacillation and recrimination came
"to an end, and it was settled that the colonies shall under-
"take to keep up their self-defence, as well as the duties of
"self-government, the obstacles to a cordial understanding
"rapidly disappeared. Canada in particular has shown a
"high, generous public spirit, which Lord Dufferin has

"known how to cultivate and guide. The sentiment of
"loyalty, not only to the monarchial principal, but to the
"person of the Sovereign, which has always been powerful
"in Canada, is now freed from any alloy of suspicious dis-
"satisfaction with the policy of the Colonial Office. It is
"not forgotten how fervid was the enthusiasm with which
"the Prince of Wales, some years ago, was received by the
"Canadians. The Princess Louise is certainly not wanting
"in the winning qualities which distinguishes members of
"the Royal House. But in truth there is no need to specu-
"late upon the influences of individual character. For the
"great body of Canadians, it is enough now that the
"daughter of the Queen is among them, holding her Court
"in her Mother's name. They will finally rid themselves
"of the lurking, haunting suspicion that, as Colonists, they
"are poor relations of the Imperial household. The task
"which the Marquis of Lorne has undertaken does not re-
"quire great powers of statemanship in the ordinary sense
"of the term, but calls for a great combination of qualities,
"which no man can summon to his aid at will. Lord
"Dufferin was a model Governor-General of Canada. His
"cultivated intelligence, disciplined by practical experience
"of public affairs at home, was stimulated by a quick
"imagination, which gave breadth and warmth of colour to
"his oratory. Yet his tact, his balance of judgment, his
"strong sense of equity, his fine temper, were never found
"wanting. The first duty of a Colonial Governor is to hold
"himself above and away from local politics. But his
"second, and hardly less important, duty is to avoid
"chilling sympathies, hurting the susceptibilities of the
"people by a too rigid reserve. Lord Dufferin steered
"clear of excess in both particulars. The Marquis of Lorne,

"however, has great advantages in attempting the same
"career. His wife's exalted rank will naturally raise him
"high above the level of local intrigues, and will at the
"same time prevent condescension from having inconve-
"nient consequences. The principal functions of Governor-
"General of Canada is to keep alive a sense of real and
"intimate connection between the colonists and the mother
"country. The colonists cannot doubt that such a connec-
"tion exists when they see among them one of the Princesses
"of the royal family of England. The Governor-Generalship
"opens a care to Marquis of Lorne that may be some com-
"pensation for political activity from which his marriage
"cut him off at home. He is well-known, intelligent,
"cultivated, with an interest in the Colonial Empire of
"England, of which he gave proofs from his early travels
"and writings, he inherits the political reputation of one
"of the governing families of Great Britain, and in Canada
"so abundantly peopled by Scottish settlers, his being the
"heir of the Macallummore will count for a good deal. But
"the most significant consequences of the Marquis of
"Lorne's appointment will be, if we are not mistaken, the
"effect of public opinion in Canada of its bare announce-
"ment. It will be hailed, we have no doubt, as the most
"popular act of policy the Imperial Government has ever
"carried out since the Dominion was founded."

The Toronto (Ont.) *Mail*, representing the great Liberal-Conservative party of that Province, gave unmistakable utterances of approval:—" The young Lord who will now,
"as the head of the Canadian Government, represent the
"Queen, has had great advantages. He is the son of a
"distinguished statesman, the Duke of Argyll. He has
"himself been for many years in Parliament. He is a

" scholar and an author of some distinction. He is a per-
" sonal friend of the Governor-General, whose intimacy with
" his family our picture galleries have attested, and he will
" have the benefit of Lord Dufferin's experience and advice.
" He brings with him a Princess whose taste and talents
" and charms of mind and person have won for her a high
" place in the hearts of the English people. With fine
" natural gifts, with more than the ordinary culture of
" educated men, with the experience of a politician, with,
" moreover, the mistakes and successes of many predecessors
" before him, Lord Lorne will enter on his vice-regal duties
" with the happiest auguries. Nor among these must be
" placed as least the fact that he comes among a people on
" whom no amiable or brilliant quality will be lost."

The Montreal *Herald*, in commenting on the appointment, not only endorses the new Governor-General, but hints at some not impossible results which may follow the residence of the Queen's daughter in Canada :—" We are
" sure that there will be a general feeling of satisfaction at
" the announcement which reached us by telegram yester-
" day morning, that the Marquis of Lorne is to be our next
" Governor-General. The loyalty of Canadians of all classes
" will be gratified at knowing that they are to have for the
" representative of their Sovereign one who is related to
" her by a close family tie. They will be proud to have
" among them a daughter of their Queen, and be glad to be
" thus assured that Her Majesty has a new and personal
" concern in the welfare of this part of her Dominions.
" Their affectionate loyalty will be warmed by this ad-
" ditional bond between Her Majesty and her transatlantic
" subjects ; and they will find reason to hope that the direct
" interest which Her Majesty will now have in Canada may

"contribute to increase even our material prosperity. There
"can be no doubt that the residence at Ottawa of a son-in-
"law of the Queen, and of one of the Princesses of the royal
"house, will attract a great deal of attention to the Domin-
"ion, and probably thus do much to further the great
"public enterprises which we have in hand. The prevail-
"ing sentiment, however, will not turn so much on possible
"but contingent material benefits, as upon the pleasure
"that will be derived from the proof thus afforded of the
"reality of the connection between Canada and the Empire.
"It is not unlikely this appointment may lead to a change
"in the character of our Government, and that, instead of a
"Governor-General, we may hereafter have a real Vice-Roy,
"with a more permanent tenure than that of our Governor-
"General. The Marquis is not an old man ; nor has he at
"present had much opportunity for a display of statesman-
"ship, but he comes of a family of distinguished statesmen,
"none of whom have, for many generations, fallen away
"from those principles of civil and religious liberty, for the
"maintenance of which one of them fell a martyr. All the
"traditions of his family should make him a conscientious
"man and a constitutional ruler. We have every reason
"to believe that he will not bely the noble race of which he
"is a descendant."

We have quoted extensively from the opinions expressed by the Canadian and English press on the appointment of the Marquis, partly because it will be a source of gratification to His Excellency and his Royal Consort, to know with what warmth of approbation the announcement of their coming to Canada was received, and mainly because these editorial opinions are of historic value.

CANADA—POLITICAL SITUATION.

The appointment, by Lord Beaconsfield, of the Marquis of Lorne as our Governor-General, involving as it does, the residence in Canada for a considerable period of a member of the royal family, constitutes an epoch in the history of our country. This remarkable period has been hastened by the course of events during the past decade in the various English-speaking countries. We, as Canadians, have contributed most to the result referred to by what we have failed to do.

This epoch is one in which the commercial and political attitude of the Dominion will be considerably altered. Our position will no longer be that of uncertainity. In the very nature of the events now transpiring we shall be compelled to define our position, at least commercially. Our connection with the mother country must be strengthened and better understood, or broken off altogether. If the latter, it will be through the persistent mismanagement of British statesmen, which alone was responsible for the loss of the American colonies in 1776. We do not, however, greatly fear the results. Unless there be continued timidity and indecision at Ottawa; unless there be a failure at the last moment in England, and unless we still suffer ourselves to be robbed by American statesmanship, Canada will soon pass from the commercial bondage in which she has been so long held, and enter upon a period of comparative commercial independence.

One of the first things we need is a complete understanding with the Home Government, and it is not impossible that this may come too late. We are either a part of the British Empire, or we are not a part of it. If the former, as we have supposed our success is the success of the Empire at large, and any commercial policy which the Government of this country may adopt, suited to our needs as a distinctive part of that Empire, cannot mean disloyalty. We have always desired to discriminate in favour of British products, and Canada has now a long standing offer of differential duties in favour of England and our sister colonies, upon the conditions only that the mother country and the other colonies will discriminate in our favour in return.

England is now proclaiming, officially and through her press, against the signs of protection in Canada. She has been well satisfied with the commercial policy of Canada for the past five years and, it seems, would have us continue it in the future. And yet what do we learn concerning this policy by an examination of the trade returns. Our imports from Great Britain, which in 1873 were $68,522,776, fell in 1877 to $39,572,239, a decline of nearly one-half in the brief space of five years ; while on the other hand, our imports from the United States increased from $47,735,678 to $51,312,669. This is the very condition of our trade to which England objects, and which Canada desires to overcome. But in respect of our exports, while in 1873 we exported to Great Britain $38,743,848, and in 1877, $41,567,-469, we exported to the United States in 1873 $42;672,526 and in 1877 only $25,775,245. In 1877 our imports from the United States were double the value of our exports to that country, which if taken into consideration with the almost par values of the currency of the two countries and the great difference in the tariff rates will indicate our loss and their gain during that year. In the same year our exports to England exceeded in value of our imports from that country by two millions of dollars in round figures. Hence it can be seen at once that the Canadian commercial policy which England has tacitly approved, taken in consideration with that of our neighbors, works the result of making Canada a market for American producers, and England a market, to some extent, of Canadian products. It would be more to the credit of the English journals which have been so loud in denouncing expected Canadian protection of late, were they to become better acquainted with the simplest facts in the case at issue.

We do not write as Conservative or Reformer. In party issues we have no interest; to party doctrines we owe no allegience. These are questions far above the ownership of any party. It was the late Prime Minister's misfortune— the country's misfortune—that he was pledged to principles of free trade for Canada, and it will for some time to come, remain a profound mystery that a statesman of his great ability should persist in promulgating a semi-free trade policy in the very face of the ruin it was working to the country. The country never lost confidence in his honesty of purpose, in his purity of character; but it was to the credit of the intelligence of the Canadian people that his fiscal policy was condemned at the polls at the recent general election; and as admirers of the Honorable Mr. Mackenzie we earnestly hope that future developments may place the personal responsibility of the fiscal policy of his Government upon the shoulders of the honorable gentlemen who presided at the department of finance, in such a manner as to show that the Premier was not personally guilty of pursuing it to his fall.

We have heard much about a "national policy," but beyond what ideas the term suggests to our mind we have nowhere seen or heard an exposition of what it is or is to be. We look in vain among the speeches, editorials, pamphlets, and what not, of the recent political campaign to find the terms and doctrines of this policy set forth. We have read the able pamphlets of the Honorable Senator Macpherson, but these are devoted mainly to an attack upon his political foes. With some slight exceptions we cannot say anything better for the speeches of Sir John A. Macdonald or the Honorable Dr. Charles Tupper. The speeches of the Honorable James Macdonald and Thomas White, Esq., M.P., have afforded us a little light, but a complete investigation of the campaign literature of 1878 yields no real exposition of the national policy. This fact is not without great significance. It shows plainly that the national policy sentiment which is being developed in Canada is not the product of any single mind, nor, indeed, the property of a political party. It is the outgrowth of our political system; the result of the high tariff policy of our neighbours; the spontaneous growth of untrammelled free speech. It was not planned, formulated and promulgated by Sir John A. Macdonald or any other Canadian statesman; but that shrewd party leader was the first to detect its young life in the pulse beat of the country; and, seizing upon it as a battle cry, it is not strange that he thrilled the whole country, leading his followers, through personal defeat, to complete party victory. Had Mr. Mackenzie been the tactician that his great opponent is; had he possessed sufficient foresight to have discerned the signs of the times, and displayed sufficient elasticity to have conformed to the popular will, his party might have championed a noble cause in a new lease of power. But we have no fault to find that the destinies of the national policy have fallen into Liberal-Conservative hands.

But what is this national policy of Canada to be? The answer has not yet been defined. It would be presumption in any one to undertake, just now, a satisfactory definition; for, as we have observed, it is not a mere party policy. It is the voice of the peculiar attitude of the Dominion Confedracy, a voice which has sounded in the ears of Canadian statesmen for the past eleven years—ever since the union of 1867—without making itself understood. Our politicians, having been educated under the old regime, could not discern the wants of the new situation. Our Confederation birth-rights made us commercially a nation, but we would not realize the blessings consequent upon the change; and it stands to the discredit of every statesman in Canada, that our fiscal policy has been what it has for the past eleven years. We have been imitating the Mother Country as if the fiscal policy of England would apply to Canada; and all the while England was craftily seeking protection to her manufactures through a confessed free trade policy.

We do not pretend to any great political knowledge, and will not undertake to say what the Canadian national policy ought to be, but there are some things which may be considered in connection with the present peculiar attitude of the country which ought to guide the new government in framing its fiscal policy. A national policy to be worthy of the name must arrest the flow of our population to the United States. And we venture the assertion that any policy which fails to do this will not satisfy the country.

The last census of the United States showed that about 500,000 *native born* Canadians were living in that country. These figures do not include the vast number of those who have come to Canada from European countries, and, being dissatisfied with the prospect which this country afforded them, passed on to the States. If we add to the latter the multitude which have left our shores since the last United States census was taken, we may safely place the total at over 150,000. This is certainly a very deplorable part of the history of Canada; and yet we have men upon whom the title of Statesman seems to fit comfortably, telling us, in effect, that Canada is to rise and prosper while this continues. In short we must conclude that the policy of our government for the past ten years—whether Conservative or Reform—has been unsound and unwise, even to driving away from the country the most enterprising youth of the land ; and what can be more injurious to Canada than the expatriation of its youth which is yearly sapping the vitality of the people.

We must not expect all our young men to become farmers; and the best sermons which we may be able to preach on the great dignity and honor of that occupation will not accomplish any such result. It is not desirable that it should. The Canadian young men of to-day are in happy contrast with their predecessors of, say, twenty-five years ago. Education has taken the place of ignorance among the masses, and the great variety of professional occupations, are prepared for and sought after. What shall these young men do ? The reply is found in our history. Failing to find suitable occupations in Canada they forsake it, painful though it may be, and seek, in a foreign country, to find employment according to their tastes. And by what manner of policy is this to be overcome? It would seem that a policy which makes the United States a market in which our youth are sacrificed, would, if rightly applied to Canada, afford them an ample variety of profitable and suitable occupations at home. We have heard much boasting of our natural resources, of our healthy climate, and maritime position. Our lack of prosperity does not, therefore, consist in the want of these things. We have all the elements necessary to a sound and permanent national growth, and yet our development has been slow and unsatisfactory. The fault lies in the incapacity of the Canadian Government.

Let us for a moment glance at the trade and industries of the Dominion in their connections with England and the United States and see, if we can, how it would be possible for Canada to carry out free trade principles in her fiscal policy without the most ruinous consequences. And we must remember at the outset that almost, if not all Canadian statesmen have at some time in the past embraced decided free trade doctrines. This has been one of our misfortunes. We have done but little independent thinking, adopting for the most part, the theories advanced by English leaders. England has been, essentially, a free trade nation, and Canada has adopted the same policy so far as it was possible for the country to do so and raise the necessary revenues; and for no good reason beyond a loyal tendency to imitate the mother country. Hence we find, when the National policy begun to make friends, that its advocates recorded, in advance of their support, an apology for the cause which they were about to pursue. They could not deny their political faith in the past and were unwilling to confess themselves to have been mistaken. One instance of this is furnished in the opening remarks of Senator Macpherson's recent address at Walkerton, Ont. " I may tell you," he says, " that I, myself, have been a free trader. I would be so to-day if our neighbors would reciprocate." And yet in the course of the Honorable Senator's address he proves himself a champion of protection. To say that he would be a free trader under a reciprocity is a positive contradiction, for who does not know that a well adjusted reciprocity treaty with the United States, would be a kind of protection to Canadian industries. Whenever we can secure proper protection, whether by tariff or treaty, we shall be quite willing that our friends may call it *free trade*, or by any other name they chose, but it will be protection all the same.

A great many things have transpired to deceive us in our relations with the United States. From 1854 to 1865 we had moderate protection in a Reciprocity Treaty with that country. When that treaty was abrogated our real position was disguised by the war prices which ruled there, and which, so long as this continued, afforded us more protection than we enjoyed under reciprocity. But these did not continue, and our industries have consequently suffered. Our manufacturers found it impossible, with the disadvantages under which they labored, and with their products excluded from the United States by a protective tariff, to compete with their rivals from that country who are permitted to bring their products into Canadian markets at very low duties. The manufacturers of the United States have therefore had a monopoly of their own market of forty millions of consumers, and a slaughter market of four millions in the Dominion.

We do not seem to realize that the greater part of the

CANADA—POLITICAL SITUATION.

natural products of the United States are admitted to the markets of this country free of duty, while the same articles produced in Canada are subject to a high duty when taken to that country. This statement is amply demonstrated by the following figures :

	Canadian Duty.	U. S. Duty.
Wheat	Free	20c. per bushel.
Rye and Barley	Free	15c. do.
Indian Corn and Oats	Free	10c. do.
Wheat Flour	Free	20 per cent.
Rye Flour and Cornmeal	Free	10 per cent.
Oatmeal	Free	$\frac{1}{2}$c. per lb.
Live Animals	10 per cent	20 per cent.
Salt	Free	In packages 12c. per 100 lbs.; in bulk 8c. per 100 lbs.
Wool	Free	25 to 50 p. c.
Pig Iron	Free	$7 per ton.
Bar Iron	5 per cent	35 to 75 per cent.
Plate and Boiler Iron	5 per cent	$25 and $30 per ton.
Iron Rails	Free	$14 per ton.
Steel Rails	Free	$25 per ton.
Bricks	Free	20 per cent.
Trees, Plants, and Shrubs	10 per cent	20 per cent.
Flax, dressed	Free	$40 per ton.
Flax, undressed	Free	20c. per bushel.
Flax Seed	Free	$20 per ton.
Starch	2c. per lb	1c. per lb. and 20 $ cent. *ad valorem*.

Canada admits all of the following undermentioned articles at the general duty of 17½ per cent., while the Americans tax the same articles, if exported from Canada to their markets, at the following rates :—

Wood Screws	56 to 60 per cent.
Saws	40 to 50 "
Cars and Locomotives	35 "
Machinery	35 "
Stoves and other iron Castings	30 "
Woollen Cloth	66 to 70 "
Flannels and Blankets	85 "

Ready-made Clothing	35 to 60 per cent.
Carpets	50 to 84 "
Alpaca Goods	85 "
Heavy Cottons	40 "
Finer Cottons	50 to 70 "
Cotton Yarn	46 to 60 "
Spool Thread	47 to 81 "
Silk Cloths	50 to 60 "
Linen Cloths	30 to 40 "
Rubber and Leather Goods, Fur Goods, Glass Bottles and Lamp Chimneys, Clocks, Furniture, Carriages, Envelopes, Writing Paper, Room Paper, Felt Hats of wool, Guns, Rifles, Pistols, Umbrellas and Parasols	35 "

It is somewhat provoking to hear certain Canadian journals tell their readers that the United States has ruined her own industries by this high tariff, and that the depressed state of business generally in that country has been produced by the same policy. Such language in the United States would be evidence of the grossest ignorance. It may be claimed that protection in that country has caused overproduction, but this is an evil which must result in the greatest harm to the manufacturers themselves. But overproduction is not a permanent evil. Indeed, if viewed as a temporary evil it has its advantages, and will always adjust itself.

There are those in this country who persist in making the mistake of " pooling " the tariff and financial questions of the United States. This has been carried so far that some of the leading journals have endeavored to show that protection for Canada means all sorts of inflation. It would be difficult to conceive of anything more stupid than this, but newspapers of respectability are found which undertake to show by a course of arguments that such will be the results. A journal which has gained a high place in the estimation of the Canadian people for the ability of its editorials has just been brought to our notice, using this language: "The very aim of protection, namely to fill the land with operatives with no stake in the country, is laying the foundation for the next step in the Communistic direction, namely, the sham money movement. The proposal has been already made, in a very irresponsible quarter it is true; but were the proposer of it as crazy as Kearney he would find followers." We do not see the force of this argument, except it means that Canada must not be to the inconvenience of maintaining operatives though the refusal be at the expense of her prosperity. On the very same line of argument, the Gospel should not have been sent to the heathen, since it increases his responsibility. It is not difficult for an unpartisan mind to discern in such nonsense as this the plainest traces of political dodgery.

But we have a word to say to those who have erroneously come under the impression that the fiscal policy of the United States has produced the hard times now distressing that nation. If this theory be true, then Canada may take to herself the credit of having made the discovery; for, as yet, no such idea is entertained by our neighbors. There is a belief current among them that manufacturers have been suffering from over-production, caused by the high protective tariff, but the very low prices at which American manufactures are sold, consequent upon this so-called evil, more than compensates, in some quarters at least, for the evil itself. But over-production is not regarded in the United States as a very serious evil; nor do the statesmen of that country attribute, in any serious degree, the recent hard times from which the country has suffered, to the high tariff policy of the Government. On the contrary, it is a realization shared in by the great mass of the American people that, with the unparalleled civil war debt, under which every industry has been sorely taxed, had the government not resorted to the most positive protective tariff, complete national bankruptcy must have been the result. But, instead, observe what has been achieved. Not many days ago an item travelled the rounds of the Canadian press informing us that the United States was the only nation of the globe whose exports exceeded her imports. We, who have become acquainted with the industries and institutions of that country by actual observation, can appreciate the value of their fiscal policy, and sympathize with the down-trodden manufacturers of Canada, who, with only here and there a miserable exception, have lost their money and wasted their energies.

The Americans are not such fools as we sometimes take them to be, and we cannot afford to judge of them always by the measure of their wild financial theories. We must at least give them the credit of having outwitted us in almost everything except the Fishery Award, and, unless they turn out to have more honesty than we usually credit them with, they may defeat us in this also. One thing is pretty certain: if they were being ruined by a high tariff, there would soon be heard the cry of free trade from the Atlantic to the Pacific. But what are the facts? At the last session of Congress it was sought to elicit an expression on the tariff, and for this purpose a bill was introduced to modify the rates imposed and to adopt as nearly as possible a uniform rate of thirty-five per cent.—just double the Canadian tariff. It is needless to say the measure was not entertained for a single moment.

In looking at the Canadian fiscal policy it is not difficult to observe its weakness, and to discover how it came to pass that our Finance Minister was astounded with so many deficits. The duties under our tariff are levied on the *ad valorem* plan, that is the duty of every $100 worth of imports is, if at the rate of 17½ per cent., $17.50. Hence with the decline in the value of imports there was a corresponding falling off in the revenue realized. What was to be done? Protection or a higher tariff could not be tolerated; but the Government did that which is far worse. Money was borrowed to cover these deficits, on which, of course, interest has to be paid; and this very interest has to be paid by the consumers, and ultimately the principal also. Now, can there be any advantage in this course? Certainly not. It is a system of giving the consumer credit by the weak contrivances of a Finance Minister. Yet this is just what has been done in Canada. And it will be most charitable to presume that such a course was adopted partly because the Finance Minister was unable to discover the cause of the deficits. It will thus be perceived that over-production in the United States—which has caused the decline in the value of our imports—worked quite as much injury to this country as it did in the United States, but all owing to our own stupidity, for we ought to have been the gainers by this decline in the market prices of our American imports.

These things show us plainly that our prosperity is governed chiefly by the fiscal policy of our neighbors, and by the policy which we bring to bear upon theirs. We do not intend to say that we must be governed by their policy, but we do say that upon their policy depends, or ought to depend, the terms of our own. They are the greater, we the less. If we disregard their policy as we have done for years, we must continue to suffer adversity. Both political parties are alike guilty in this respect, and whatever we have said respecting the past policy of our Government it applies with equal force to every year since Confederation. Had the same policy, touching our trade relations with the United States, which characterized the Government the first five years after Confederation, been applied to the last five years, the results could not have been different. It is well that protection has now been taken up as a party measure, and whether secured by a reciprocity treaty or a reciprocity tariff, we sincerely hope it will be secured.

Under existing arrangements our industries must remain prostrate. They can offer no safe investment to capitalists. Our own market is limited and must remain so until our population is increased, and this can be accomplished only by furnishing profitable employment in a wider variety of occupations than we now represent, and by expanding those which are now struggling for an existence. To increase the one will be to enlarge the other. "The market in the United States is large, " but the Canadian is practically excluded from it by " the protective tariff of that country. Now, if capital- " ists contemplated establishing manufactures on this conti- " nent, would they not be more likely, under existing " circumstances, when the cost of the raw materials and of " the elements that go to make up the cost of manufactures, " including labor, is about the same in both countries— " would not thoughtful, prudent moneyed men be more " likely to establish their industries on the other side of the " line in the midst of forty millions of people, and from " whence they could enter when they chose the more " limited Canadian market at comparatively low rates of " duty and trample upon the Canadian manufacturers?

CANADA—POLITICAL SITUATION.

" Would they not rather do so than invest their capital in
" this country, in the midst of four millions of people,
" knowing that, if they wished to take their manufactures
" to the larger market on the other side of the line, they
" would be met by duties so high that, when they paid
" them, they would be unable to compete with the manu-
" facturer in the United States; and in addition to this
" would be exposed to crushing competition in the limited
" home Canadian market." This is not only our present
condition, but it has been the disadvantage under which
Canada has always labored.

Producing as little as we do—and it is a wonder we have
not produced less—our importations are so large that all
we produce and export is insufficient to pay for them and
the interest on the public debt of the Dominion, and on
other indebtedness, such as loans, provincial, municipal, etc.
In short, the amount of obligations for which the country
has to provide is greater than its products are sufficient in
value to meet. " The balance of trade," justly observes the
Honorable Senator Macpherson, " is against us, that is the
" value of our imports over the value of our exports for the
" ten years between in 1868 and 1878 amounted to the
" enormous aggregate sum of $236,000,000. The balance
" of trade, like many commercial questions, is one about
" which much is written by theorists, and these gentlemen
" would have us believe that our prosperity is not affected
" by the fact that our imports largely exceed our exports.
" I contend that that is a dangerous fallacy in this country.
" It is different in England, where, according to the official
" returns, the imports are larger than the exports, but
" England carries on an enormous indirect foreign trade;
" English capital is invested in every civilized country, and

"the interest on foreign investments and profit on her in-
"direct trade, items which do not appear in the Trade
"Returns, are more than sufficient to adjust the balance in
"her case. We have little or no indirect trade, no foreign
"investments, and no means of meeting our engagements
"—no means of paying for what we import, except with
"the products of the soil, the sea, the forest, and the mine.
"We have nothing but our natural products to export, and,
"therefore, if what we produce in that way is insufficient
"to pay for our importations and the interest we have to
"remit to our creditors, then we are rolling up a debt
"against ourselves."

The views of Senator Macpherson, above quoted, are not dissimilar to those recently expressed by an able English writer. He observes :—"Canadian trade figures, taken
"generally, have for long given unmistakable signs that
"her business on the whole was not following its natural
"course. Canada has been importing beyond her means
"year after year, or at all events much beyond her export-
"ing capacity, and no doubt she has been able to do so by
"reason of the money which we had so freely lent her. A
"new, raw, unopened country, can have no margin to trade
"upon in this fashion, except by borrowing, and it follows,
"therefore, that so far as our business with Canada has been
"based on money lent beyond the true capacity of the
"country to pay the loans, it has been misused, and must
"be reduced. Since 1873, a process of reduction has been
"going on, which is, therefore, so far healthy ; but the
"limit is, I am persuaded, not yet reached, especially as
"the exporting capacity of the Dominion has, at the same
"time, been on the decline. What the healthy basis may
"be it would be hard, in view of the facts I have indicated,

"to predict; but it is quite clear, when we consider the
"large sum which the country has yearly to find for in-
"terest on Government loans and on dividends in companies
"working with foreign capital, there can be no safety till
"the export figures are in excess of the import.   *   *
"Wait till the tide has well turned, and then we shall see
"what the wealth of the farmer means. He stands to be
"ruined by a big crop in Europe or America. What Canada
"has most of, beef, pork, corn, wood, and wool, the United
"States has a great deal more of herself, and what the
"United States seeks to supply in the shape of manufactures,
"Canada wants to make at home. There is hence no good
"scope for a large development of reciprocal trade between
"these two countries at present, least of all a good outlook
"for the farmer in the event of a succession of splendid
"harvests."

Here is a blow at reciprocity itself, and it is not given unguardedly. It is true that reciprocity would be an improvement on the present policy, but even such a boon would still give Americans a great advantage over us.

We have briefly considered our trade relations with the United States and will now review, for a minute, the condition of the same relations with England. England is spoken of as a free trade country, and free trade principles have certainly found the ablest advocates there, but it will be remembered that notwithstanding this England is far from being a free trade nation. She collects from her customs duties about $100,000,000 annually. But while we admit that England is largely a free trade country, we, at the same time, claim that this policy has always been pursued by the mother country as a policy of indirect protection. It was a scheme of the British Government to pro-

tect British industries and to secure to their manufacturers a monopoly of the markets of the world. In 1846 when the late Sir Robert Peel introduced his bill to the British Parliament to abolish duties on raw materials, breadstuffs, etc., he used language which plainly indicates the real object of so-called English free-trade. He said: "In the year
" 1842 it was my duty, as the organ of the Government, to
" propose a great change in the then existing customs of the
" country. The general plan upon which I then acted was
" to remit the duties upon articles of raw material, con-
" stituting the elements of manufacture in this country.
" The manufacturers of this country have now, therefore,
" an advantage which they have not hitherto possessed.
" They have free access to the raw materials which con-
" stitute the immediate fabric of their manufactures. They
" wished to establish the prosperity of that great staple
" manufacture of this country—the cotton manufacture—on
" some sure and certain foundation.

"Sir, I propose, in taking the review of duties still exist-
" ing to which we are invited by Her Majesty, to continue
" to act upon the principle which this House has sanctioned,
" and I take in the first instance those articles of raw
" material which still remain subject to duty. I mean to
" deal with them in order still further to enable me to call
" on the manufacturer to relax the protection he still en-
" joys. Sir, there is hardly any other article of the nature
" of a raw material which is now subject to duty. I pro-
" pose, without stipulation, that England should set an ex-
" ample by a relaxation of those heavy duties, in the confi-
" dence that that example will ultimately prevail; that the
" interests of the great body of consumers will soon in-
" fluence the action of the Governments, and that by our ex-

"ample, even if we don't procure any immediate reciprocal
" benefit, yet, whilst by a reduction like that we shall, in
" the first instance, improve our own manufactures, I be-
" lieve we shall soon reap the other advantage of deriving
" some equivalent in our commercial intercourse with other
" nations. I do hope that the friends and lovers of peace
" between nations will derive material strength from the
" example which I have advised, by remitting the impedi-
" ments to commercial intercourse. But observe, if that be
" the effect, I think in all probability that the continuance
" of permanent peace will expose us to a more extensive
" and more formidable competition with foreign countries
" with respect to manufactures. During war we command-
" ed the supply of nations. Peace has introduced not only
" new consumers, but also formidable manufacturing in-
" terests. In order that we may retain our pre-eminence, it
" is of the greatest importance that we neglect no opportu-
" nity of securing to ourselves those advantages by which
" that pre-eminence can be alone secured. Sir, I firmly
" believe that abundance and cheapness of provisions is one
" of the constituents by which the continuance of manu-
" facturing and commercial pre-eminence may be obtained.
" You may say the object of these observations is to flatter
" the love of gain, and administer merely to the desire of
" accumulating money. I advise this measure on no such
" ground. I believe that the accumulation of wealth, that
" is the increase of capital, is a main element, or at least
" one of the chief means by which we can retain the pre-
" eminence we have so long possessed."

In the light of this language of one of the founders of English free trade, it is not difficult to see that the whole scheme was in the interests of British manufacturers. Sir

Robert Peel recognized that nothing contributes so much to the wealth of a nation as pre-eminence in manufactures, because a nation that manufactures even enough for herself retains within her own borders the wealth produced and created there, except so much of it as she must give in exchange for what she requires and cannot produce and manufacture. "The money which changes hands for what is "produced in the country remains in the hands of the "people of the country, and is not sent abroad to enrich "other lands. When Great Britain opened her markets to "the world, her far-seeing statesmen expected that other "nations would accept the principles of free trade, follow "her example and abolish their protective duties. But the "statesmen of France, Germany, Belgium, Switzerland, "and other European countries were far-seeing also. They "recognized the fact that without manufactures they could "not become wealthy and powerful, and they adhered to a "protective policy. The United States did the same. The "result has been that the manufacturers of those countries "have not only retained a large share of their own markets, "but have been enabled to compete with the manufacturers "of Great Britain in the other markets of the world, and "latterly even to compete with them at home, to some ex-"tent, and now we find many of the British mannfacturers "looking for protection from the competition of their "foreign rivals." So that we see that free trade has not accomplished for Great Britain what was hoped for it by its projectors. The United States is to-day successfully competing with English manufacturers on English soil, and we all know that in Canada American manufacturers has almost taken the place of English.

It is easy, indeed, to be in favor of free trade. There is

not a sensible man in Canada who is not to day *in favor* of free trade for Canada, but from whence is this free trade to come? Canada will be one of the parties to the compact—what country will be the other? for, verily, it requires two parties to this compact, as to all others. We are all in favor of free trade. The trouble is to find the same favor among those with whom we desire to have this trade. What we are not in favor of is the giving of free trade to our neighbours by our statesmen, while they fail to obtain it in return for this country. Free trade, pure and simple, would be Reciprocity pure and simple, an untaxed exchange of commodities. When this cannot be secured, we must take the only sensible alternative,—a reciprocity of tariffs. The cost of producing the commodities of the United States and Canada is about equal, hence when the United States imposes a higher duty than Canada upon the same articles it taxes the industry of this country more than its own is taxed by us. It is quite plain, therefore, that the industries of Canada are suffered to be taxed by the United States.

Wherever a nation has been deceived by free trade doctrines, or entered into a free trade that was not fully reciprocal, it has been attended with the same results. Prince Bismarck's words are here given in evidence of this: " I " have given free trade a trial, and it does not seem to have " benefitted the country commercially, industrially, or " financially. I am overwhelmed with lamentation re-" specting the decline of trade and the decay of manufac-" turing enterprise, and with assurances—from people for " whose judgment in such matters I entertain the highest " respect—that partial and moderate protection will remedy " those evils as if by magic. Therefore, I also propose to

"give protection a chance of ameliorating the condition of
"the manufacturing and operative classes, and of lightening
"the load which the budget unquestionably lays upon the
"shoulder of the nation. As certain of the Ministers with
"whom I have hitherto worked on my former platform will
"not range themselves by my side on my new platform, I
"must rid myself of them, and put others in their place who
"will carry out my resolves."

Our policy towards the United States should be a decisive one. We have vacilated so long that they will now have but little confidence in our professions; and we shall not be able to extract terms from them by anything short of decisive action, and, very probably, even that will have no avail under the circumstances. It has been suggested by one that we should meet them on this ground: "We
"have offered to exchange with you, on a free basis, the
"commodities which we both produce; we would prefer
"that reciprocity to any other—that is, an absolutely un-
"taxed exchange of commodities; but, as you refuse to
"enter into such a treaty with us, then we will adopt your
"policy. As you will not give us untaxed reciprocity,
"we will reciprocate tariffs. That is the language we
"ought to use to them—not in a spirit of retaliation at all,
"but simply in the interest of Canada."

It may be that this would satisfy most of the Canadians, but we should have but little confidence in such a policy, only in so far as we depended upon the Americans to refuse reciprocity. It has always appeared to us that a reciprocity with the United States is not what Canada requires. Such a policy is nothing more or less than commercial annexation, to be followed, if long continued, by political annexation also. But, aside from its political significance, its commercial disadvantages are quite enough to condemn it. Experience ought to teach us. We have had reciprocity, and what did we gain by it? Is it not true that our national prosperity has been delayed immeasurably by that treaty? It taught us to depend for everything we needed upon the American producer, and when the treaty was ruthlessly abrogated what was our condition? It was well understood by the Americans, and their only disappointment was that we were not then compelled to seek relief in immediate annexation. It was a crisis in the political history of Canada. England saw it, and despaired of our continuing to be much longer a profitable British colony. There are many of us who will not soon forget the tone of the English press and of the English government on that occasion. It was hinted, in no very unmistakable language, that we might set up for ourselves, or sell ourselves out, or do most anything by which England might be relieved of us. Finally, Confederation was devised, partly to resurrect our fallen and decayed industries. This step was wholly unexpected by the Americans, and they derided it, just as now they are deriding the signs of a coming national policy. And why? Because that, like the proposed new policy, was calculated to save us from the evils of annexation.

We now venture to predict that if the in-coming Parliament adopts a decisive reciprocity of tariffs with the United States, it will produce in a short time, overtures from that country for a reciprocity treaty. Not because the Americans can derive anything commercially from such a treaty, for they cannot, but because of prospective political gains. The motive which actuated the United States in making the old treaty was the acquisition of Canada. If they shall desire to renew it, it will be from the same motive; and it will be an evil day for Canada when her statesmen consent to another reciprocity treaty with the United States. It does not require extraordinary penetration to decern a feeling of general disappointment among the American people in relation to this country. It was first caused by Confederation; then Lord Dufferin's anti-American sentiments increased it; finally, the appointment of Lord Lorne and his Royal Lady provoked it to open confession. Until recently Canada had been slowly but surely drifting into the American Republic through the medium of commercial intercourse. But during the last ten years we have not made much advancement in that direction, and recently we have assumed an attitude which, if maintained, will save us from such a fate altogether. But all these good influences and wholesome measures would be more than counteracted by a few years of commercial annexation, such as we should experience under a renewal of reciprocity.

It would seem that the true fiscal policy for Canada would be that of Reciprocal tariffs with the United States now and forever, with differential duties in favor of England and English colonies. We must develop and foster an inter-British trade. Give us Reciprocity with England, and tariffs stout and strong with our neighbours. Whenever we shall conclude to become a political constituent of the United States, as Professor Goldwin Smith would have us do, or whenever we adopt the other policy of political Independence, or if we intend to take either of these steps in the future, then a Reciprocity Treaty with the United States will be a legitimate and profitable investment for the country, but so long as we profess to foster British connection such a thing must be antagonistic with our destiny. For one, the writer must denounce as productive of great evil to Canada, any policy or measure which tends to weaken our connection with the Mother country, or to strengthen the chances of converting us into a constituent part of the American Republic. And it must be admitted that the policy and measures of our Government for the past ten, or even twenty years, have not been wholly free from such a tendency. Therefore we say, in conclusion, that our new national policy will not deserve the name, if it does not embrace:—

I.—Reciprocity of tariffs with the United States, not for purposes of revenue, or to secure a renewal of Reciprocity Treaty, but primarily to protect Canadian industries.

II.—Differential tariff in favor of England and the English colonies with a similar policy on the part of England and the English colonies in favor of Canada.

III.—A closer connection with the Mother Country commercially and politically.

And we do not think that if, in carrying out the third article of this policy, our Dominion should graduate into an Empire sufficiently perfect to admit of a Viceroy instead of a Governor-General, and that a member of the Royal family should be sent to exercise vice-regal rule over us permanently, it would be among the worst things that could happen to this country. It would certainly be greatly to be preferred to annexation with the United States.

THE DOMINION CABINET

AND

ADMINISTRATOR-GENERAL

1878.

GENERAL SIR PATRICK L. MACDOUGALL,

ADMINISTRATOR-GENERAL.

THE interregnum in the administration of the Governor-Generalship, between the departure of Lord Dufferin and the arrival of Lord Lorne, has, in accordance with constitutional usage, placed the responsibility of the station upon the Commander of the Forces in Canada, viz., General Sir Patrick L. Macdougall. Consequently, that distinguished officer demands more than a passing notice in our little volume. He was educated at the Royal Military College, and joined the 79th Highlanders at the age of 16 years. He served afterwards with the 36th Regiment in New Brunswick, having come to Quebec in the " Pique " frigate with the late Lord Sydenham, and having been afterwards sent with despatches overland from Montreal to Halifax in December, 1840, for a great part through a country almost destitute of roads. He served as Captain and Major with the Canadian Rifles in Canada from 1844 to 1854, when he was appointed Superintendent of the Royal Military College at Sandhurst. At the formation of the Staff College—which was constituted very much on a plan of his own—he was appointed the first Commandant in 1857. From 1865 to 1868 he served as Adjutant-General of Militia of Canada during the period which was troubled by the foolish and wicked proceedings of the " Fenian Brotherhood," and assisted in organizing the Militia of the Dominion after Confederation. From 1870 until he was transferred to the command of the forces in Canada he was employed at the War Office, during the last five years with the intelligence department, of which he was appointed director on its first formation. He is the author of the following military books :—" Theory of War," " Modern Warfare," and the " Campaign of Hannibal," as well as of the biography of General Sir W. Napier, the distinguished author of the Peninsular War. He was employed on particular service in the Crimea in 1855, and has the Crimean and Turkish medals. He received the honor of Kt. C. M. G. in 1877.

RIGHT HON. SIR JOHN A. MACDONALD, K.C.B.,

PREMIER AND MINISTER OF THE INTERIOR.

The name of this great statesman has become so closely identified with that of the Dominion of Canada that the two are almost synonymous. His public career is interwoven with our history for the last quarter of a century, so closely that it is impossible to find a political measure which is not in some degree a representative of the man, either in his advocacy or opposition of it. He has been a wonderful manager, and is acknowledged to be the greatest statesman in his party, if not in the whole country. He was born January 11, 1815, and is the eldest son of the late Hugh Macdonald, Esq., of Kingston, Ont., formerly of Sutherlandshire, Scotland, where, we believe, Sir John was born, he emigrating to this country with his parents at the age of three years. This, however, is disputed by some, who claim that he is a native Canadian. We have applied to the Right Honorable gentleman for certain information required to perfect this sketch, but he has extended only a polite refusal to be in any way instrumental in aiding us, until his next retirement from office. For this we are unwilling to wait, and, being quite familiar with his public record, from our labors in compiling the history of Canada, we will undertake to produce a brief sketch of the Chieftain, notwithstanding, to use his own language, "A complete biography has never been written."

We cannot, this minute, cite our authority, but give it as a reliable item of history that the great statesman was born in Scotland. He was educated at the Royal Grammar School, Kingston, Ont., under Dr. Wilson, a Fellow of Oxford University, and was called to the bar of Upper Canada in Hilary Term, 1836. Ten years later he was created a Queen's Counsel. A naked skeleton of his public life may be thus sketched :—He was a member of the Executive Council of Canada from May 11, 1847 to March 10, 1848 ; from the 11th of September, 1854, to 29th July, 1858 ; from 6th August, same year, to 23rd May, 1862 ; and from 30th March, 1864, until the Union, and was during these several periods Receiver.General from 21st May to 7th December, 1847 ; Commissioner of Crown Lands from latter date to 10th March, 1848; Attorney-General for Upper Canada from 11th September, 1854, to 29th July, 1858, when as Prime Minister he and his Cabinet resigned, being defeated on the Seat of Government question. He was returned to office 6th August the same year, as Postmaster-General, a position he resigned the following day, on his re-appointment as Attorney-General of Upper Canada, which he continued to hold until the defeat of the Administration on the Militia Bill, in May, 1862, when he and his colleagues again retired from office. Sir George E. Cartier and he led the Opposition in the Assembly, until the defeat of the Sandfield Macdonald-Dorion Government, when the Tache-Macdonald Government was formed, 30th March, 1864, and he returned to his old office of Attorney-General, and was Government leader in the Assembly from that time until the Union of the Provinces, 1867. He held the office of Minister of Militia Affairs jointly with that of Attorney-General, from January to May, 1862, and from August, 1865, until the Union. He was requested to take the place of Sir E. P. Tache, as Prime Minister, on the death of that gentleman in 1865, but waived his claim in favour of Sir N. F. Belleau. He has been a delegate to England and other countries on public business on many occasions, and was a delegate to the Conference in Charlottetown in 1864, which had been convened for the purpose of effecting a Union of the Maritime Provinces; to that which succeeded it in Quebec in the same year, to arrange a basis of Union of all the British American Provinces, and was Chairman of the London Colonial Conference, 1866-7, when the Act of Union, known as the "British North America Act," was passed by the Imperial Parliament. On 1st July, 1867, when the new constitution came into force, was called upon to form the first Government for the new Dominion, and was sworn of the Privy Council, and was appointed Minister of Justice and Attorney-General of Canada. In 1871 he was appointed one of Her Majesty's Joint High Commissioners and Plenipotentiaries, together with Earl de Grey (now Marquis of Ripon) Sir Stafford Northcote, Sir Edward Thornton and Right Honorable Montagu Bernard, to act in connection with five Commissioners named by the President of the United States, for the settlement of the Alabama claims, and of matters in dispute between Great Britain and the United States, the labours of which Joint High Commission resulted in the Treaty of Washington, signed at Washington, U.S., on 8th May, 1871. He received the degree of D. C. L. (honorary) from Oxford University, 1865. Is also an L.L.D. of Queen's University, Kingston. He was created K. C. B. (civil) by Her Majesty, July, 1867. He was created a Knight Grand

Cross of the Royal Order of *Isabel la Catolica* (of Spain), January, 1872. He was appointed a member of Her Majesty's Most Honorable Privy Council, July, 1872. He sat for Kingston in the Canada Assembly from November, 1844, until the Union. Returned to Commons, 1867, and again in 1872, 1874, and 1875. Sir John A. Macdonald's legislation amongst many other important public measures, includes the following :—The secularization of the clergy reserves ; the improvement of the Militia laws ; amendments to the law relating to the jurisdiction and procedure of the Surrogate Courts ; abolishment of imprisonment for debt in certain cases ; prevention of preferential assignment to creditors ; amendment of the jury law ; amendment of the election law ; improvement of municipal institutions in Upper Canada ; the consolidation of the statutes ; the extension of the municipal system ; the reorganization of the militia; the settlement of the Seat of Government question; the establishment of direct steam mail communication with Europe ; the establishment of additional penitentiaries, criminal lunatic asylums and reformatory prisons, and providing for the inspection thereof; the providing for the internal economy of the House of Commons ; the reorganization of the Civil Service on a permanent basis ; the construction of the Intercolonial Railway ; the enlargement of the canals ; the ratification of the Washington Treaty ; the Confederation of British North America and the extension and consolidation of the Dominion. At the recent general elections Sir John was defeated in Kingston, but was immediately afterwards elected by acclamation in Marquette County, Manitoba.

Now, this brief summary covers a period of more than forty years of active life, and would require a volume more than five times the size of the present one, to set forth in any degree of detail. But this is not all. In 1873 the Pacific Railroad developments decided him and his colleagues to resign office. He was then Premier, and had been the leader of the Government since 1867. On the succeeding day he was elected leader of the Opposition, and since that time has labored indefategably until in the present year he has been restored to power.

Sir John married Miss Clark, of Invernessshire, Scotland, who died in 1856. In 1867 he married Miss Barnard, daughter of the late Hon. T. J. Barnard, of Jamaica. Among the Freemasons he has been very prominent, being at present Grand Representative in Canada of the Freemasons in England.

Sir John A. Macdonald is one of those few men who wins the admiration of his political foes, as the following from the Montreal *Star*, a journal bitterly opposed to him in the recent contest, will show: "In appearance though by no "means so stoutly built, Sir John A. Macdonald somewhat "resembles Lord Beaconsfield, like whom, when occasion "demands, he has the same ability to submit himself to cir-"cumstances, make the best of a bad job, and though sorely "beaten carry himself with a jaunty if not a defiant air. "There have been those who described him as 'devil-may-"care.' About him there is a remarkable amount of "animal magnetism, his personal popularity being almost "unbounded; had it not been for which, and his great abili-"ties, he could not so soon have made headway against the "defeat which he righteously sustained in 1873. Through-"out his entire career, he has been ambitious; some will "say that his first care was to distinguish himself, and "secondly to promote in every way the development and

"prosperity of Canada. He is largely possessed of the lust
" of power, to obtain and retain which he has not perhaps
" been as scrupulous as he might have been, either in the
" means to which he resorted, or the pledges and promises
" which he made. He has all the necessary qualities for a
" party leader, *fortiter in re, suaviter in modo*. Of him it has
" been said that the refusal of a favor at his hands has been
" much more satisfactory to receive than a benefit at the
" hands of others. It has been his habit to be true to his
" friends, so long as they would be true to him, but the
" moment he noticed any divergence he has utilized only as
" long as he required them, and then put them to the right
" about, only to restore them to partial favor when they
" were prepared humbly and unquestionably to carry out
" his mandates, and to make as substantial amends as were
" possible for their offences against the party. Sir John is
" and has been an apt master of men. He thoroughly un-
" derstands human nature, being sufficiently astute to mani-
" pulate his followers and draw out of them the very best
" talents that they possess, and dispose of them to the best
" possible advantage. As a speaker, though not eloquent,
" he is powerful. He is given to recklessness in his state-
" ments, and few will deny that he is over sanguine in his
" anticipations.

" Upon the stump he is more than ordinarily successful,
" his quickness at repartee and his almost inexhaustible
" fund of humor making for him friends even in the strong-
" holds of his enemies. The good points which he has
" made would occupy a first-class chronicler, even of the
" Dean Ramsay school. Taking into the calculation his
" qualities of head as well as of heart—for in politics the latter
" go a long way—he is the greatest man we have in Canada,

"and if there is virtue, which there is reason to believe is
"the case, in the fiscal policy which he now champions, he
"is the man, associated with those whom he can select to
"aid him, to carry it out to success. It is, perhaps, needless
"to say that in his case, as in that of most politicians, a
"strong Opposition is required to keep him quite up to the
"mark. Where party interests are concerned, as has before
"been noticed, he is somewhat careless of the means which
"he employs to attain his ends, but, although brought face
"to face with many offences perpetrated, in the interest of
"party, it has yet to be proved that he has committed im-
"proprieties for his own personal gain and advantage.
"Since 1873 he has filled the position of leader of the Con-
"servative Opposition, at first an exceedingly small body
"that has gradually been reinforced until to-day it has with
"it in power, backed as it is by men from both sides, a
"majority that may, perhaps, be termed unwieldy, and too
"overwhelming since its members and their demands will
"be difficult to satisfy, while the mere weight of numbers,
"as has often been the case in previous Parliaments, will be
"found sufficient, at any rate for the time being, to crush
"and render of comparatively little avail any opposition that
"may be offered to them. Prior to 1873, as Mr. Mackenzie
"was accustomed to say, motions were made upon his side
"the House, not because there was any hope of carrying
"them, but in order that they might be placed on record.

"Since that time, as the Honorable Dr. Tupper ex-
"plained, motions and objections have been offered, not be-
"cause it was expected they would have any effect upon
"the House, but in order that through the House the
"country might be reached, and in both cases, that object
"was attained. Still there is great room for objection to

"election speeches being made in the Legislative Halls,.
"where the time of the members and of the country might
"be much better occupied in practical legislative work. In
"the public interest we say it is to the general regret that
"the incoming Government should go in having so immense
"a following. Defeated at Kingston, which he had repre-
"sented for almost thirty-five years, Sir John Macdonald,.
"by the courteous withdrawal of both the candidates in the
"field, was elected by acclamation for the County of Mar-
"quette, Manitoba, and on assuming office he obtained the
"endorsation of himself and policy by the electors of the
"city of Victoria, British Columbia."

Sir John A. Macdonald has formed the subject of many newspaper sketches. The New York *World* recently said of him among other things, "A portrait of Disraeli would find ready sale in Canada as a life-like likeness of the 'Knight of Kingston.'" Slightly above the medium height, slim, irreproachably dressed and buttoned up, close-shaved, pale and rather sallow, with dark hair and eyes, a prominent nose that looks a little Oriental at the nostrils, and a curl that "hangs right down on his forehead." The resemblance is remarkable, and Sir John has been thought not to be wholly unconscious of or indifferent to this fact. Sir John walks with a semi-limp and has hardly aged perceptibly during the last twenty years. He is a clear, easy and unaffected speaker, best in debate, but no orator as McGee was. Per- sonally, he is a charming companion, witty, agreeable and caustic with a fund of anecdote. Lady Macdonald is much younger than her husband, to whom she is devoted, and her tact and fascination it is said prove powerful aids to him. At some future time, whenever convenient opportunity pre- sents itself, the writer contemplates giving the public a complete history of the life and public services of this truly great statesman.

He is once more at the head of the Government, this time as Premier and Minister of the Interior, and is far more popular with the Canadian people to-day than ever before. It is hinted by some of his friends that in the not distant future he will retire from public life in Canada and remove permanently to England. However this may be, and in whatever capacity he may chose to labor, we must hold the opinion that his active political life will not soon close, and that the near future will open to him honors greater than any which he has yet enjoyed. It is not impossible that he should yet become a peer of the Realm. Such an event would rejoice Canada greatly.

THE HONORABLE SAMUEL LEONARD TILLEY, C.B.,

MINISTER OF FINANCE.

OUR present Finance Minister is one of the foremost statesmen of the Dominion. It is difficult to say whether there are two or only one in his party who can justly claim precedence to him. Sir John must always be acknowledged chief, but after him, we must not undertake to say who should rank first. This honor, however, lies with one of two men, viz., the Honorable S. L. Tilley and the Honorable Doctor Charles Tupper. No doubt there are many Nova Scotians and New Brunswickers who, at the risk of antagonistic political elements, look forward expectantly for a Tupper-Tilley or Tilley-Tupper Government. It is to say the least a matter upon which we Maritime people have a right to pride ourselves that, excepting Sir John, we are represented by the two ablest statesmen in the Dominion of Canada. And if at any time either of these gentlemen should be incapacitated we have the Honorable James Macdonald, who would take the place of either, and of whom many predict a career quite as brilliant as that of the great chieftain himself.

Mr. Tilley has made a grand record as a public man. His abilities have placed him in the very foremost ranks of every enterprise or measure of his province for the past quarter of a century; and his great purity of character, to-

THE DOMINION CABINET. 167

gether with his noble efforts as a reformer, have gained for him a host of friends and admirers of both political creeds in every province of Canada, and in most of the States of the neighboring Republic. In the cause of Total Abstinence and Prohibition Governor Tilley, as we have accustomed ourselves to call him, has been one of those few men who could triumph in an unpopular cause.

A condensed summary of his public career may be thus sketched. He is a son of Thomas M. Tilley, Esq., of Queen's County, N.B, and great grandson of Samuel Tilley, Esq., formerly of Brooklyn, N.Y., a E. U. loyalist, who came to New Brunswick at the termination of the American revolution, and became a grantee of the city of St. John. He was born, at Gagetown, Queen's County, N.B., 8th May, 1818, and educated at the County Grammar School. He was a member of the Executive Council, of New Brunswick, from November, 1854, to May, 1856, from July, 1857, to March, 1865, and again from April, 1866, until the Union, during which several periods he held the office of Provincial-Secretary of that Province; and from March, 1861 to March, 1865, was leader of the Government. He has been leader of the Liberal party in New Brunswick for a lengthened period. He has been a delegate to England on several occasions to confer with the Imperial Government on important public business, notably regarding the Union of the British American Colonies and the construction of an Intercolonial Railway. He has also repeatedly served on like missions to the sister Provinces. He was a delegate to the Charlottetown Union Conference, 1864; to that in Quebec the same year, and to the London Colonial Conference, to complete the terms of Union of the British North American Provinces, 1866-7. He holds a patent of rank and precedence from Her Majesty as an Ex-Councillor of New Brunswick. He was created C. B. (Civil) by Her Majesty in 1867. He was sworn of the Privy Council, 1st July, 1869, and held the office of Minister of Customs from that date until the 22nd February, 1873, when he was appointed Minister of Finance. He was acting Minister of Public Works from November, 1868, to April, 1869. He sat for the city of St. John, in New Brunswick Assembly, from June, 1854, to June, 1856, when he was defeated on the Prohibitory Liquor Law question and the Government resigned; from June, 1857, to March, 1865, when defeated on the Union policy of his Government; and again from 1866 until the Union, when he resigned to accept a seat in the Commons and represent New Brunswick in the Dominion Cabinet. The Prohibitory Liquor Law of New Brunswick was the work of Mr. Tilley as a private member. Amongst other measures of importance introduced and carried by the Government, of which he was a member, may be mentioned as follows :—Vote by ballot and extension of the franchise; an Act authorizing the construction of the European and North American Railway as a government work; an Act authorizing the construction of the Intercolonial Railway, New Brunswick. He continued to represent the city of Saint John in the House of Commons until November, 1873, when he retired on his appointment as Lieutenant-Governor of New Brunswick. He discharged the duties of the latter post until October, 1878, when he was appointed Finance Minister on the return to power of Sir John A. Macdonald.

THE HONORABLE CHARLES TUPPER, C.B., M.D., L.R.C.S.,

MINISTER OF PUBLIC WORKS.

THE Province of Nova Scotia, though small both in area and population, has produced several very distinguished men. Haliburton as historian and humorist occupies a permanent place in English literature. Sir Edward Belcher stands high as a scientific Arctic explorer. Sir Samuel Cunard's reputation is co-extensive with the commerce of England and America. Sir Fenwick Williams and General Inglis occupy a high place as military commanders. Dr. Dawson is recognized as a worthy successor of Lyell, Murchison and Buckland. In politics, the eloquence and ability of Joseph Howe are admired far beyond the limits of his own province. All these men, whose name and fame are familiar wherever the English language is spoken, were Nova Scotians.

The Hon. Dr. Tupper, who has sought and found distinction in the arena of politics, though still comparatively young as a public man, has won a high position as one of the leading and most influential statesmen in the Dominion of Canada. He was born at Amherst, a town on the line of the Intercolonial Railway, in the County of Cumberland and Province of Nova Scotia. The family belonging originally to Hesse-Cassell, went to the Island of Guernsey, from which a branch of it emigrated to Virginia. At the time of the revolution Dr. Tupper's ancestors having adhered to the loyalist cause, removed to Nova Scotia. The Tupper family are connected with that of Sir Isaac Brock, the distinguished British officer who fell fighting bravely at the head of his troops, on Queenstown Heights. The Hon. Charles Tupper, is the eldest son of the Rev. Dr. Charles Tupper, of Aylesford, and was born in July, 1821. He was educated at Horton Academy, and is an M. A. of Acadia College. Having chosen medicine as a profession, he finished his studies at the University of Edinburgh, where he took the degree of M. D., and also obtained the diploma of the Royal College of Surgeons. In 1843 he returned to his native country and commenced the practice of his profession, in which, at an early period, he obtained a high reputation. In 1846 he married Miss Frances Morse, belonging to a leading family, and for twelve years was engaged in building up his reputation as a skilful and successful physician.

He was on the highway to professional fame and an ample fortune, but the bent of his mind lay strongly in the direction of public life, and, in 1855, he gave way to his inclination. During this year a general election took place and two members had to be chosen for the County of Cumberland. The Hon. Joseph Howe, who was at that time at the height of his fame, had been one of its representatives and was again a candidate. His seat was looked upon as practically unassailable; but Dr. Tupper nevertheless determined to enter the list against so redoubtable a champion. It seemed a truly forlorn hope, as he had to face and fight the most eloquent and popular man in the Province, and one besides who was skilled beyond most people in the wiles and devices of carrying a successful election. Mr. Howe looked upon the opposition as a sort of political impertinence and treated it accordingly. But when his youthful opponent, on the day of nomination, began to speak, it very soon became apparent that the political Goliath had met a David, and that the contest was going to be a serious one. The great Liberal leader found himself assailed with an eloquence equal to his own and a torrent of invective that carried all before it. Howe felt and confessed that a new power had made it appearance in the public arena, and though beaten this time, his opponent would be heard of again, and in due time take his place among the foremost public men of Nova Scotia. But he was not beaten, for the evening of election day found his name at the head of the poll. The venture was a daring one, and showed at the outset of his career the real stamina that was in him and which has been found to form so large an ingredient in the character of the subject of our sketch.

In 1856 Dr. Tupper took his seat in the House of Assembly and soon proved that in debating power, in political and administrative ability he was second to no one in it. At that time, the amount of first-rate talent in the House was very remarkable. Besides Mr. Howe, the Liberal phalanx included Sir William Young, Judge Wilkins, the late James Uniacke, the present Governor Archibald, Judge McCully, Judge Henry and a cloud of minor lights. The Hon. J.W. Johnston led the Opposition, a man of commanding intellect and great dignity of character. But he stood almost alone, so that the accession of Dr. Tupper was an immense gain to the Conservative party.

The public questions of the day were of an exciting character, including a proposed prohibitory liquor law, vote by ballot, an elective Legislative Council, and the abolition of the monopoly in the mines and minerals of the province. In the discussion of these questions Dr. Tupper took a leading and enegetic part, and even at this early period his views were in advance of the Liberal party as regarded liberal legislation. He advocated the principle of an elective Legislative Council in a speech of great force and eloquence, but this as well as the other measures mentioned, were for the time being defeated.

The session of 1857 brought matters to a crisis. The Government came to an open rupture with the Roman Catholics and the Liberal administration fell. In the new Cabinet formed by Mr. Johnston, Dr. Tupper filled the important office of Provincial Secretary. Measures of great and permanent interest to the country were at once introduced and carried through with remarkable energy. Dr. Tupper, though not the leader, was the leading spirit in the new Government. The elective Council bill was passed by the Assembly, but rejected by the Upper House. An Act for the final settlement of the long agitated question regarding the mines and minerals became law, by which a large monopoly was put an end to and important industry opened up to the whole community. A bill for an improved jury law was prepared by Dr. Tupper and passed about this time; and also an act making population the basis of representation in the popular branch was passed. The initiation of money votes by the government, for the first time adopted, and a bill disqualifying subordinate officers of the Crown from sitting in the legislature was introduced and became law.

In the general election of 1859 the government party was defeated and Dr. Tupper again took his seat on the Opposition benches, and remained there for four years.

THE DOMINION CABINET. 173

During the last session of this Parliament the Liberal party forced a bill through the House narrowing the elective franchise. It was fiercely opposed by the Opposition, but in vain. Its effect, however, was the complete route of its supporters at the next election. This was in 1863, when Dr. Tupper took charge once more of his former department, and subsequently on the elevation of Mr. Johnston to the position of judge in equity, the government—a position he held without a break till the confederation of 1867.

This period of four years was one of great political energy and progress in Nova Scotia. The provincial railway was extended to the Pictou coal fields, a length of 50 miles. A government subsidy was granted to a company to build a railway from Windsor to Annapolis, passing through the garden of the province, the length of the road being 85 miles. Besides these important measures Dr. Tupper prepared and passed an act for collecting the vital statistics of the province; an act for appointing a judge in equity; a new representation bill; an Act prohibiting dual representation. But the crowning Act of all, and which will hand down his name to unborn generations, was the bill giving a free education to every child in the province. The measure was much needed, but till now no minister had ventured to grasp it, fearing the consequences, as it introduced the principle of direct taxation, a course which, however wise and just, was certain to bring a storm of angry obloquy on its authors. He foresaw all this, but stood firm to his purpose. It was the most unpopular measure, perhaps, ever passed in the Provincial Parliament—an unpopularity which was only beginning to die away in 1867. Its value now is recognized as priceless, and the people would part with it upon no consideration. With characteristic intrepidity Dr. Tupper stated again and again that it might, and probably would, cost him place and power, but that he would ever regard it as one of the proudest acts of his public life. The value of the boon may be estimated from the fact that while in 1861 only 31,000 children, between 5 and 15 years attended school, the number in 1871 was upwards of 90,000. One man had the courage to fight and master a great and growing evil, the blight of ignorance covering a whole province, and he has his reward in the consciousness of having initiated and carried out successfully a noble national undertaking, making posterity his debtor.

The great question of Colonial Union was now beginning to assume a practical shape. In 1860 Dr. Tupper delivered a lecture in St. John in favor of a union of British North America, which was afterwards published and exercised a large influence upon the public opinion. In 1864 he carried a motion in favor of a Maritime union in the House of Assembly, in a speech of great force and eloquence, and organized in conjunction with the government of New Brunswick and Prince Edward Island, a delegation to consider that question. This conference took place at Charlottetown, but upon the application of a delegation from the Canadian government, agreed to take up the larger question of a union of British North America. This discussion of this proposal created great excitement in Nova Scotia, which was increased by the hostile position taken by Mr. Howe.

It is impossible to enter into details here. The anti-unionists demanded that the question should be settled by an appeal to the people. This Dr. Tupper resented, feeling, we presume, from the combined opposition to the measure, and the influence of the still odious school act, that its defeat at the polls would be certain. The motion for union was accordingly carried in the House of Assembly by 32 against 16 votes. The opposition, however, did not end here. Mr. Howe continued to agitate, to speak and write against it, both in England and Nova Scotia. He was ably answered by Dr. Tupper in an elaborate pamphlet, published in London, proving by extracts from speeches, lectures and despatches, that Mr. Howe himself had in former years been the most eloquent and earnest advocate the cause of union ever had.

The controversy ended in the ratification of the scheme of union by the Crown and its cordial acceptance by nearly every public man of eminence belonging to all parties in the Dominion. But the change produced great bitterness of feeling in Nova Scotia, and at the election for the new Dominion Parliament only one unionist was returned from that province, that one being Dr. Tupper, who has been elected nine times in succession by his native county, a strong proof of his popularity where he is best known.

The situation was now grave and the attitude of Nova Scotia threatening, but the unselfishness of Dr. Tupper in refusing office and the wise policy of conciliation and forbearance adopted by the Dominion Government conquered the difficulty and removed the danger. He was the only representative of union from Nova Scotia, but though a seat in the Cabinet and the chairmanship of the Intercolonial Railway Board were both offered him, they were declined, and it was not till 1870 that he accepted the position of president of the Privy Council. In 1872 he became Minister of Inland Revenue, and in 1873 Minister of Customs.

In the Dominion House of Commons, Dr. Tupper took

his place at once in the front rank among its leading members, a position he has continued to maintain and strengthen. On his own side of the House he stands next to Sir John A. Macdonald, whose right arm he is, and the head of a future Conservative government he is in all human probability destined to become. If the question were asked as to who are the two ablest men on each side of the House, the line is so clearly drawn that 99 out of 100 would reply without hesitation, Mackenzie and Blake on the one, Sir John Macdonald and Dr. Tupper on the other. Dr. Tupper has reached his present position through no extraneous influence. All that he has and is he owes to himself. He took his place in the front rank as a public man at the outset by pure force of character and strength of intellect. As a politician he has throughout been consistent and progressive, generally taking counsel with himself rather than following the suggestions of others. There is nothing mean, shifty or vacillating in his character. In every line of action he has taken, he followed it out in a firm, fearless and undaunted spirit. With strong party feelings and a still stronger will, his course has always been shaped in accordance with what he believes to be the public interest. In the earlier part of his career he was dreaded for his terrible powers of invective. That power remains, but he as long ceased to wield it as a weapon of offence.

The leading qualities of his mind are affluence and accuracy of language, strength of will, tenacity of purpose, clearness and rapidity of thought and promptness of action. His public speeches are an index at once of the character of his intellect and his constitutional temperament. His words are poured out like an ocean, but you will listen in vain for either verbiage or repetition. The sentences flow on keen and incisive, copious in fact and illustration, bristling with argument, and crushing in force and vigor of expression. As a debater he is, perhaps, the foremost man in the House of Commons. His articulation is clear and resonant, his utterance rapid and impassioned. But though vehement enough in manner when heated by debate, he seldom loses temper or forgets the conventional courtesy due to an opponent. His judgment is calm and collected at all times, and few can parry a thrust more adroitly or are more formidable in attack. His powers of memory, like those of Macaulay, are remarkable, so that facts, arguments and illustrations are always at his command, and are sent home with an effect that never fails to tell upon his audience. Like nearly every man who has risen to eminence in public life, detraction and calumny have followed every step in his career. Anonymous assailants have thrown at him the vilest language. These he has disdained to notice, but wherever or whenever a charge or insinuation has been openly made he has met it on the instant and crushed the life out of it, to the confusion of his assailant.

Dr. Tupper is still in the prime of life, vigorous alike in mind and body. He is a man of fine presence and intrepid bearing, with features indicating firmness and decision of character. His manner is frank, easy and cordial; his speech, whether in debate or conversation, earnest and animated. As a public man, he is one of the greatest powers in the House of Commons, and is probably destined to wield a still greater and wider influence as a Dominion statesman.

The Hon. Charles Tupper was created a C.B. (civil) by Her Majesty in 1867, in recognition of his public services;

is a governor of Dalhousie College, and was president of the Canada Medical Association from 1867 to 1870, when he declined re-election from pressure of public and official duties. He is now Minister of Public Works.

LIEUT.-COL. THE HONORABLE LOUIS F. R. MASSON,

MINISTER OF MILITIA AND DEFENCE.

'The subject of this sketch is a very interesting representative of French politeness and manners, combined with a peculiar English style characteristic of the educated French Canadian people. His worthy father, Honorable Joseph Masson, was one of the most enterprising and successful merchants of his time, and left a respected as well as popular name throughout Lower Canada. His brother, the late Honorable Edouard Masson, sat for several years in the Legislative Council of Quebec, and was a favorite with his colleagues and the public generally.

The Honorable Mr. Masson inherited the good humor and kind regards which were peculiar to his father, and it has often been observed that, whilst in the heat of debate in Parliament, how cautiously he would parry an argument and strike his opponent a blow without creating the least ill-feeling. Sir George E. Carter used to say of him that " he will make a mark; he may be my successor even, for he does not take the halter; he is sufficiently undisciplined to make a good officer hereafter." And it may be added to this that Sir George and Mr. Masson were always on the best of terms, and paid each other many marks of respect, which have not been forgotten in Parliamentary circles. But it must not be supposed that M. Masson and Sir George always agreed in their political views; but noble men, of independent characters, if prompted by a patriotic and generous spirit, can disagree on such matters without destroying their friendship for each other.

M. Masson was born in Terrebonne on the 7th of November, 1833, in the old seignorial house. He spent his early years amongst people who spoke only French. He was sent to the Jesuit College of Georgetown, and to Worcester, Mass., to commence his education. He thus acquired that knowledge of the English language which enables him to speak and write it equally as well as that of his mother tongue. To complete his education, he returned to Lower Canada and made the full course of the St. Hyacinthe College. During that period he made a trip to Europe under the guidance of the Most Reverend M. Désaulniers, a learned and very highly esteemed priest, who took him through the most important parts of the old world, such as the Holy Land, etc. M. Masson afterwards made other trips to Europe, and sometimes wrote articles for the French reviews published in the Province of Quebec These were interesting descriptions of his voyages, and always reflected much credit on the author of them.

M. Masson married Mlle. Louisa Rachel Mackenzie, daughter of Lieutenant-Colonel Alexander Mackenzie, and grand-daughter of the Honorable Roderick Mackenzie, a partner in the Northwest Fur Company, and a member of the Executive Council for Lower Canada.

He was admitted to the bar in 1859, and soon began to take a deep interest in the politics of the country. But he soon made himself known in another respect—as one of the promoters of the militia organization. His efforts in that direction were productive of the best results that could be

THE DOMINION CABINET.

arrived at. His first commission in the volunteer force is dated October, 1862. A few months later, August, 1863, he was appointed Brigade Major, a position which he held until 1868. It was during that period that he twice served (March and January, 1866,) on the frontier, against the Fenians. In the following year, 1867, he was promoted to the rank of Lieutenant-Colonel.

In the meantime confederation having become an accomplished fact, he was returned to Parliament by acclamation for the county of Terrebonne, and from that day his popularity in his native county has not in the least declined. Moreover, as his name became more and more identified with public matters in Parliament, the Province of Quebec has for several years looked upon him as its chieftain. Already, in 1873, he had refused to enter the Cabinet, on account of the unsettled state of the questions of amnesty for political offences in Manitoba, and of the New Brunswick separate schools.

When the last general election took place the French Conservative party claimed him as their leader. He was in Europe at the time; but Sir John A. Macdonald awaited his return before completing the Quebec section of his Cabinet.

M. Masson has expressed a desire on various occasions that this country might obtain a reciprocity treaty with the United States on fair and equal terms; and that he is in favor of a moderately protective tariff. He will support a scheme for constructing the Northern Pacific Railway wholly on Canadian soil, as soon as the finances and circumstances of the country will permit of its execution.

THE HONORABLE LOUIS HECTOR LANGEVIN, C.B.,

POSTMASTER-GENERAL.

The Honorable M. Langevin is one of the leading French-Canadian statesmen of the Dominion—perhaps the foremost of his party. His record for the past twenty-five years is interwoven with the most stirring political events of the country. He is a son of the late John Langevin, Esq., formerly Assistant-Civil Secretary under the Earl of Gosford and Lord Sydenham, during the periods those noblemen held the office of Governor-General. His mother was the late Sophia, Scholastique La Force, whose father, Major La Force, went with his militiamen to the frontier in the war of 1812, and whose grandfather was acting Commodore of the British fleet on Lake Ontario during the American revolutionary war. He is brother of His Lordship the Right Reverend Jean Langevin, Bishop of St. Germain de Rimouski. He was born in the city of Quebec, August 25, 1826, and educated at the Seminary of that city. He was married in 1854 to Justice, eldest daughter of the late Lieut.-Colonel Charles H. Tetu, J.P. He studied law first with the late Hon. A. N. Morin, and afterwards with the late Hon. Sir George E. Cartier, and was called to the Bar, Lower Canada, October, 1850. He was created a Q.C. 30th March, 1864. He was editor of the *Melanges Religieux* (Montreal) from 1847 to 1849, and also of the *Journal d'Agri-*

culture (same city) ; and at a later period (1857) of the *Courrier du Canada* (Quebec). He sat as a member of the City Council, Quebec, for some years, and was Chairman of the Water Works Committee. He was Secretary-Treasurer and afterwards Vice-President of the North Shore Railway Company. He was Mayor of Quebec from January, 1858, to January, 1861, and during his incumbency visited England on matters affecting the city finances, etc. He was for two years, 1861 and 1862, President of St. Jean Baptiste Society (Quebec) ; and in 1863 and 1864, President of the *Institut Canadien*, (same city.) He is author of *La Canada, ses Institutions*, etc., a prize essay (Quebec, 1855), and of *Droit Administratif ou Manuel des Paroisses et Fabriques* (do., 1862.) He was a member of the Executive Council, Canada, from 30th March, 1864, until the Union ; and held the offices of Solicitor-General, Lower Canada, from 30th March, 1864, to November, 1865 ; and Postmaster-General, from latter period until the Union. He was sworn of Privy Council, 1st July, 1867, when appointed Secretary of State of Canada, in which office he remained until transferred to the Public Works Department, 8th December, 1869. He was, while at the State Department, *ex-officio* Registrar-General of Canada and Superintendent-General of Indian Affairs. He was a Commissioner to assist Mr. Speaker in the management of the interior economy of the House of Commons ; also a chairman of the Railway Committee of the Privy Council. He was created a Companion of the Most Honorable Order of the Bath (civil) by Her Majesty, 1868. He was created Knight Commander of the Roman Order of Pope St. Gregory the Great, 1870. He was a delegate to the Charlottetown Union Conference, 1864 ; to that in Quebec in same year ; and to the London Colonial Conference, 1866-7, to complete terms of Union of British North American Provinces. In 1871, at the desire of the Privy Council, he visited British Columbia with the view of acquiring a knowledge of that new Province in relation to the Pacific Railway and its western terminus, and also of studying the requirements of the Province, and ascertaining personally what public works were necessary for it. On his return he published a report, containing much information about British Columbia, and making known its present position and immense wealth and resources, (Ottawa, 1872.) He acted as leader of the Lower Canada Conservatives in the session of 1873, during the absence to England of Sir George Cartier, and was selected by the Conservative members, after Sir George Cartier's funeral in Montreal in June, 1873, as the Conservative leader in the Province of Quebec. He sat for the County of Dorchester in Canada Assembly, from general election, 1857, until the Union. Returned to Commons by same constituency from the Union until 1874, when he retired. He ceased to be a Cabinet Minister with his colleagues in November, 1873. He also represented Dorchester in Local House from general election, 1867, to general election, 1872, when he was returned for Quebec Centre by acclamation ; he retired January, 1874 ; but was again elected for Charlevoix, January, 1876 ; and again returned for same constituency, April, 1877, after being unseated on petition. At the late election he was defeated in Rimouski County. On the return of Sir John A. Macdonald to power he was appointed Postmaster-General.

THE HONORABLE JAMES MACDONALD, Q.C.,

MINISTER OF JUSTICE.

WE never hear the name of this honorable gentleman spoken except with some remark complimentary of his great talents, and probable future distinction. That he has already taken a place in the very front ranks of his party there can be no question. His ability has few equals in the Commons House of Parliament, and it is recognized on every hand that he is one of the most promising statesmen in his party. It is thought by some that Nova Scotia is rather small for two such men as the Honorable Doctor Charles Tupper and the Honorable James Macdonald, and it was hinted at one time that the Doctor would accept one of the many constituencies which are available to him in Ontario and give way to Mr. Macdonald, in which event he would become the Conservative chieftain in Nova Scotia, a title which may now properly apply to the Minister of Public Works. This would also harmonize with the idea, held by many, that the Honorable Doctor will succeed to the honors of Sir John on the retirement of the latter, and it must be conceded that our Premier, to be untrammelled by sectional jealousies, must come, politically, from the great province of Ontario. We Cumberland people are by no means willing to part with the Doctor, and as Nova Scotians, most of us would lose a great degree of our interest in his political welfare should he leave us. We Nova Scotians are not unlike Irishmen. We are Nova Scotians the world over. It is quite easy for a New Brunswicker or a person from Ontario, on going to the States to loose his nationality and become Americanized, both in politics and manners; not so with the Nova Scotian. There is something peculiar in his very appearance; something characteristic, but not always admirable in his accent; something in his very akwardness, if you please, which is Nova Scotian. But beyond all this, if he be a genuine Nova Scotian he is a true patriot, but not the less, for all this, loyal to the Crown. He loves his country and is not ashamed to confess it every where. But this is altogether digressing from the subject, though, perhaps, not unintentional.

The family of the Honorable James Macdonald came from the highlands of Scotland to Pictou, N. S., nearlya century ago, and Mr. Macdonald was born at East River, Pictou, 1st July, 1828. He was educated at New Glasgow, N.S., and called to the Bar of Nova Scotia in 1851. He was created a Q.C., 1867, and was Chief Railway Commissioner for Nova Scotia from June, 1863, to December, 1864, when he was appointed Financial Secretary in the Government led by the Honorable Dr. Tupper, which he continued to hold until the Union. He was one of the Commissioners (representing Nova Scotia) appointed to open trade relations between the West Indies, Mexico and Brazil and the British American Provinces in 1865-66. He sat for Pictou in the Nova Scotia Assembly from 1859 until the Union, and from the general election in 1871, until July, 1872, when he resigned. He was an unsuccessful candidate for Pictou in the House of Commons in 1867. He was first returned to Commons in 1872, and defeated in 1874. At the recent general elections Mr. Macdonald was again elected for Pictou, and was appointed by Sir John A. Macdonald Minister of Justice. Mr. Macdonald's parliamentary career has been brief, if we take into consideration the high place which he has already gained in the public estimation. He has by no means reached the zenith of his political fame.

THE HONORABLE JOHN O'CONNOR, Q.C.,

PRESIDENT OF THE COUNCIL.

THE Honorable John O'Connor, Q.C., is descended from two distinct families of O'Connors of Kerry, Ireland. His father and mother were both O'Connors, though not related within known degrees of kindred. His parents emigrated to America in 1823 and settled at Boston, where John was born in January, 1824. He settled in Essex County, Ontario, with his parents, in 1828. Choosing the profession of law he was called to the Bar of that Province, Hilary Term, in 1854, and in 1872 he was created a Q. C. He is also a member of the Michigan (U.S.) Bar, and was for a considerable period Reeve of the Town of Windsor. He was Warden of Essex County for three years, being twice elected by a unanimous vote of the County Council; and for twelve years he performed the duties of Chairman of the Board of Education of the Town of Windsor, Ontario. He is the author of " Letters addressed to the Governor-General on the subject of Fenianism (1870)." On the 2nd of July, 1872, he was sworn of the Privy Council and was President of that body until March 4th, 1873, when he was appointed Minister of Inland Revenue. He was an unsuccessful candidate for the Canadian Assembly in 1861, but succeeded in 1863 in unseating the then sitting member (Mr. Arthur Rankin) and obtaining a new election, when he was re-

THE DOMINION CABINET. 189

turned, and sat until the dissolution of Parliament in May of that year. He again unsuccessfully contested the same seat at the general election in 1864, but was returned in 1867, and again in 1872, and was again defeated in 1874. In the recent election Hon. Mr. O'Connor was returntd for Russell County. He is for the present, and has been for some time in the past, considered the chief representative of the Irish Canadians.

THE HONORABLE ALEXANDER CAMPBELL, Q.C.,

RECEIVER-GENERAL.

HE is the son of the late James Campbell, Esq., M. D., formerly of Hedon, Yorkshire, England, and was born in the East Riding of Yorkshire, in 1822. He came to Canada with his father when very young, and was educated at Lachine, at the College of St. Hyacinthe, Que., and at Kingston. He was called to the Bar, Upper Canada, in Michaelmas Term, 1843, and was created Q.C. in 1856. He is Dean of the Faculty of Law, Queen's University, Kingston, and a director of the London and Canadian Loan and Agency, and was President of the Royal Canadian Bank. He has been a Bencher of the Law Society, Upper Canada. He represented Cataraqui division in Lower Canada, from November, 1868, until the Union. He was Speaker of that body from 12th February, 1863, until the dissolution of Parliament in May of the same year; and a member of Executive Council and Commissioner of Crown Lands, from March, 1864, until the Union. He was a member of the Quebec Union Conference, and sworn of the Privy Council, 1st July, 1867, and was Postmaster-General from that date until 1st July, 1873, when he was appointed First Minister of the Interior, an office he continued to hold until the resignation of the Macdonald Government, 5th November, of the same year. He was Government leader in the Senate from 1867 until November, 1873. He proceeded as a delegate to England on public business, early in 1870 ; and again in June of the same year, to make representations to the Imperial Government, respecting injures inflicted by Fenian marauders, and the necessity for continuing a regular military force in the country. He was called to the Senate by Royal Proclamation in May, 1867. During the past five years Hon. Mr. Campbell has acted as leader of the Conservative Opposition in the Senate. On the return to power of the Conservative party he was appointed Receiver-General by Sir John A. Macdonald.

THE HONORABLE JOHN HENRY POPE,

MINISTER OF AGRICULTURE.

HE was born in the Eastern Townships, and there are no records at hand which give the date. His is President of the St. Francis and Megantic International Railway, and of the Compton Colonization Company. He is also one of the trustees of the St. Francis College, Richmond, P.Q., and a director of the Eastern Townships Bank. He commanded the Cookshire Volunteer Cavalry for many years, and retired retaining his rank as Major, in 1862. He was sworn of the Privy Council and appointed Minister of Agriculture in October 1871, which position he held until November 5th, 1873, when he retired with his chief, Sir John A. Macdonald, on the Pacific Railway question. He sat for his present seat in Canadian Assembly from 1857 until the Union. He was an unsuccessful candidate for same seat at general election in 1854, but was returned to Commons by acclamation at general election in 1867; again on his appointment to office, and again at the general election in 1872, and still again in 1874. In the recent contest the Honorable Mr. Pope was elected by a large majority. He has the unqualified confidence of his constituents, and of the country.

THE HONORABLE F. G. BABY, Q.C.,

MINISTER OF INLAND REVENUE.

THE family is one of the oldest and most honorable in the Province of Quebec, the founder of it, Jacques Baby de Rainville, an officer in the celebrated regiment of Carignan-Sallieres, having come to this country in 1663. He is a son of the late Joseph Baby, Esq., N.P., by Caroline, daughter of the late Honorable Louis Guy, in his lifetime King's Notary, and a Legislative Councillor for the old Province of Quebec; and grandson of the late Honorable Francois Baby, an Executive and Legislative Councillor, and Adjutant-General of Militia for the same Province. He was born in Montreal on the 26th August, 1834. He was educated at St. Sulpice College, Montreal, and at the College of Joliette. He was called to the Bar of Lower Canada in 1857, and was created Q.C. in 1873. He is Mayor of the town of Joliette. He was an unsuccessful candidate for Joliette at the general election in 1867. He was first returned by acclamation in 1872; and re-elected in 1874, and again at the recent general election.

THE HONORABLE MACKENZIE BOWELL,

MINISTER OF CUSTOMS.

He was born at Rockinghall, Suffolk, England, on the 27th of December, 1823, and came to Canada with his parents in 1833. He is a Major in the 49th Battalion, and a Director of the Grand Junction Railway. He is Vice-President of the Dominion Editors' and Reporters' Association, and President of the Hastings Mutual Fire Insurance Company, of the West Hastings Agricultural Society, of the Farren Manufacturing Company, and of the Dominion Safety Gas Company. He was editor and proprietor of the Belleville *Intelligencer* for a lengthened period, and has also been President of the Ontario Press Association. He was for eight years Grand Master of the Provincial Orange Grand Lodge of Quebec East. He was elected Most Worshipful Grand Master and Sovereign of the Orange Association of British America, an office he held for seven years. He is also Deputy Grand Master of the Grand Black Chapter of British America. He was an unsuccessful candidate for North Hastings in the Canadian Assembly in 1863; first returned to Parliament in 1867, and has sat for the county since that time. He was re-elected at the recent general election, and appointed by Sir John A. Macdonald Minister of Customs in 1878.

THE HONORABLE JAMES COX AIKINS,

SECRETARY OF STATE OF CANADA.

OF the many able and excellent men by whom Sir John Macdonald has been surrounded during the several times in which he has administered the Government of the country, there has not been one whose personal and political character has stood higher, or one who has evinced a more zealous devotion to the proper discharge of his public duties than the honorable gentleman whose name appears at the head of this notice, and who now, for the second time, so worthily presides over the Department of State at Ottawa. Honorable by nature as well as by the title of courtesy which he holds, Mr. Aikins bears a record such as many an older and more experienced statesman might well envy. His whole course through life has been a blameless one.

James Cox Aikins is the eldest son of the late James Aikins, Esq., a native of the County Monaghan, Ireland, who, emigrating to Canada in the early part of the present century, proceeded to the western country, where he took up land in the Township of Toronto, in what is now the County of Peel. Here the present Secretary of State was born, on the 30th March, 1823, and here he also received the primary portions of his education. In due course he proceeded to Victoria College, Cobourg, then, as now, the principal seat of learning of the Wesleyan Methodist body (to which communion the Aikins family are attached), and there remained for a considerable time. Among his classmates at this institution were Hon. William Macdougall, C.B., Matthew H. Ritchey, Q. C., now M. P. for the City of Halifax ; Lieut.-Colonel J. Stoughton Dennis, now Surveyor-General of the Dominion ; Colonel Walker Powell, the present Adjutant-General of Militia ; Hon. Senator Brouse ; J. M. Keeler, M.P. for East Northumberland ; J. L. Biggar, ex-M.P., and others who have since played important parts in the public life of the country. It may also be mentioned that his two brothers, Dr. William Thomas Aikins, now President of the Toronto School of Medicine, and Dr. Moses Henry Aikins, of Peel, were students at the same University. Returning to the family homestead, it was not long before his friends, seeing of what material he was composed, sought his services in a legislative capacity. At the general elections of 1854, having declined nomination in 1851, in response to their solicitations, he offered himself as a candidate for the representation of the County of Peel in the Legislative Assembly of the late Province of Canada, and was successful, defeating the former member, Mr. Gorge Wright, by a considerable majority. Mr. Aikins continued to represent Peel until the general election of 1861, when owing to his action on the County Town question which excited sectional oppotion, he lost his seat, the late Hon. John Hillyard Cameron, a foeman worthy of his steel, being returned as the member elect. In the following year he was elected to the Legislative Council (then an elective body) for the " Home " division, comprising the counties of Peel and Halton—his majority in Peel alone reaching over 300. Such is the inconsistency at times of electoral bodies. In the Legislative Council Mr. Aikins continued to sit, taking an active and intelligent part in the discussions, until it ceased to exist, owing to the Confederation of the British North American Provinces in 1867, when he was called to the Senate of the Dominion by the Queen's Royal Proclamation. He still continues a member of the Senate, and both as a Minister of the Crown and as a private member has taken a leading part in its business and legislation. During the past five years the Senate has rendered most useful and important services to the State, not only in acting as a check on the oftentimes crude and imperfect legislation of the Commons, but in initiating and carrying forward many measures and enquiries of great public interest. It was the subject of this sketch who unearthed and brought to light the Anglin printing scandal, the Kammistiquia and Neebing Hotel job, and the Mackenzie conspiracy to " stuff" the Senate ; and for this, if for nothing else, he is deserving of the hearty and sincere thanks of a grateful people. The present is, as we have said, the second occasion on which Mr. Aikins has filled the office of Secretary of State. He held that portfolio in Sir John Macdonald's previous Cabinet, from 9th December, 1869, up to the retirement of the Administration in November, 1873, and it was during his incumbency that he constituted and established the Dominion Land's Bureau, for the purpose of managing the vast domain in the North West then recently acquired from the Hudson Bay Company. This office has since been erected into an independent Department. Indeed, Mr. Aikins introduced the Act constituting it the Department of the Interior. Mr. Aikins also prepared, with the assistance of Colonel Dennis, the Public Lands Act of 1872, the liberal and enlightened provisions of which measure remain unaltered and intact to this day. As Secretary of State, he had then, as he has now, charge of the Queen's Printer's Office and of the Stationery Office, both of which he overhauled and remodelled with singularly beneficial results, not only to the Civil Service, but to the public exchequer, many thousands of dollars having been saved to the country annually through his economical and judicious management and care.

Mr. Aikins was first returned to Parliament as an Independent Reformer, and his whole course has amply justified the appellation, for from first to last he has taken a thoroughly free and independent attitude. His first vote, that on the Speakership in 1854, was cast against the Hincks-Morin candidate, the late Sir George E. Cartier. He also supported Sir John Macdonald's measure for the secularization of the Clergy Reserves. Since Confederation he has been a follower of the great Conservative Chieftain, and he may therefore be now classed as a "Conservative-Liberal." Mr. Aikins married in 1845, Miss Mary Elizabeth Somerset, who is also from Peel, and he is the father of several children.

THE HONORABLE JAMES COLLEDGE POPE,

MINISTER OF MARINE AND FISHERIES.

HE is the second son of the Hon. Joseph Pope of Charlottetown, Prince Edward Island, a descendant of a Huguenot family which settled in Cornwall shortly after the revocation of the Edict of Nantes. He was born at Belleque, in Prince county, Prince Edward Island, on the 11th June, 1826, and educated in England. At a partial election held in 1857 he was elected a member of the Prince Edward Island House of Assembly for Prince county, and again re-elected for the same county at the general election in 1858, and also at the general election in 1859. He was Premier of Prince Edward Island from 1865 to 1867, in which year he retired from politics, retaining by permission of Her Majesty the rank and precedence of an Executive Councillor. In 1868 he was an unsuccessful candidate for the representation of Prince county in the House of Assembly. As the advocate of a system of public instruction based on the principle of paying for results. In 1870 he was elected a member of the Prince Edward Island House of Assembly, and again became Premier. In 1871 he carried a bill for the construction of the Prince Edward Island Railway; and in April, 1872, on an appeal being made to the country, the Government was defeated. In 1873, at a general election, he was elected a member of the House of Assembly, and became again Premier, when he succeeded in carrying the resolutions under which Prince Edward Island entered the Dominion. In 1873 he resigned his seat in the House of Assembly, and was elected a member of the House of Commons for Prince county. At the general election which followed the retirement from office of Sir John A. Macdonald Government in that year, he did not seek re-election. In 1875 he was elected by acclamation to represent Prince county in the House of Assembly. In 1876 he was an unsuccessful candidate for the representation of Charlottetown in the House of Assembly. He was rejected by reason of his views upon the school question. On the appointment of the Hon. David Laird as Governor of the Northwest in 1876, he was elected to represent Queen's county in the House of Commons in the place of Mr. Laird, the city of Charlottetown giving him a majority over his opponent of 465 votes. At the last general election, in 1878, he was elected for the House of Commons for Queen's county by a majority of 889 over his opponent. He was sworn of the Privy Council and appointed Minister of Marine and Fisheries in October, 1878.

PARLIAMENTARY AND LEGISLATIVE
DIRECTORY.

N.B.—The full names of some of the Local Members could not be ascertained. The list was made up so soon after the elections that the names of subordinate officers, secretaries, etc., could not in all cases be given.

OFFICIAL DIRECTORY.

GOVERNOR-GENERAL:

HIS EXCELLENCY THE RIGHT HONORABLE JOHN GEORGE EDWARD HENRY DOUGLASS SUTHERLAND CAMPBELL, Marquis of Lorne, etc., Governor-General and Commander-in-Chief of the Dominion of Canada.
(For full title, biography, etc., see pages 111 to 125.)
☞ The Governor-General's Staff not yet announced.

MINISTER AT WASHINGTON:

RIGHT HONORABLE SIR EDWARD THORNTON, K.C.B., Envoy Extraordinary and Minister Plenipotentiary of Great Britain, Washington, D.C.
VICTOR A. W. DRUMMOND, ESQ., Secretary of Legation.

QUEEN'S PRIVY COUNCIL FOR CANADA:

(Ministry formed Oct. 21, 1878.)

RIGHT HONORABLE SIR JOHN A. MACDONALD, K.C.B., Premier and Minister of the Interior.
HON. JOHN O'CONNOR, Q.C., President Council.
 " JAMES MACDONALD, Q.C., Minister of Justice.
 " LOUIS F. R. MASSON, Minister of Militia.
 " CHARLES TUPPER, C.B., M.D., Minister of Public Works.
 " JAMES C. POPE, Minister of Marine and Fisheries.
 " SAMUEL L. TILLEY, C.B., Minister of Finance.
 " JOHN H. POPE, Minister of Agriculture.
 " MACKENZIE BOWELL, Minister of Customs.
 " ALEX. CAMPBELL, Q.C., Receiver-General.
 " H. L. LANGEVIN, C.B., Postmaster-General.
 " LOUIS F. G. BABY, Minister of Inland Revenue.
 " JAMES COX AIKINS, Secretary of State.
W. A. HIMSWORTH, ESQ., Secretary to the Privy Council.

MEMBERS OF PRIVY COUNCIL WITHOUT OFFICE:

Hon. Alexander Mackenzie.
" L. Laflamme, Q.C.
Sir Albert James Smith.
Hon. Richard John Cartwright.
" C. A. P. Pelletier.
" David Mills.
" Isaac Burpee.
" Thomas Coffin.
" Richard W. Scott, Q.C.
" Lucius Seth Huntington, Q.C.
" Wilfred Laurier.
" Alfred G. Jones.
Sir Alex. Tilloch Galt, K.C.M.G.
Hon. William Macdougall, C.B.
" William P. Howland, C.B.
" Adams G. Archibald, C.M.G.
" Peter Mitchell.
" Jean Charles Chapais.

Sir Edward Kenny, Kt.
Sir John Rose, Bart., K.C.M.G.
Sir Frs. Hincks, K.C.M.G., C.B.
Hon. Alex. Morris, D.C.L., Q.C.
" Chris. Dunkin, D.C.L., Q.C.
" Theodore Robitaille, M.D.
" T. N. Gibbs.
" Hugh McDonald, Q.C.
Sir Antoine Aime Dorion.
Hon. Donald Alex. Macdonald.
" David Christie.
" Telesphore Fournier.
" Wm. Ross.
" Felix Geoffrion.
" David Laird.
" Luc Letellier de St. Just.
" Joseph Edward Cauchon.
" William B. Vail.

Hon. R. D. Wilmot.

THE SUPREME COURT.

Sir William Buell Richards, Chief Justice.
The Honorable Samuel Henry Strong, Puisne Judge.
      "   Telesphore Fournier,   "
      "   Henri Elzéar Taschereau,   "
      "   William Johnston Ritchie,   "
      "   William Alexander Henry,   "

THE SENATE OF CANADA.

The Honorable R. D. WILMOT, *President.*

PROVINCE OF QUEBEC.

THE HONORABLES

Armand, J. F., Riv. des Prairies.
Baillargeon, Pierre, Quebec.
Bellerose, J. H., St. Vincent de P.
Bureau, Jacques O., Montreal.
Chaffers, W. H., St. Césaire.
Chapais, J. C., Kamouraska.
Chinic, Eugène, Quebec.
Cochrane, M. H., Compton.
Cormier, Charles, Plessisville.
Dumouchel, L., Longueuil.
Fabre, Hector, Quebec.
Ferrier, James, Montreal.
Guévremont, J. B., Sorel.
Hamilton, John, Montreal.
Lacoste, Louis, Boucherville.
Paquet, A. H., St. Cuthbert.
Pelletier, C. A. P., Quebec.
Penny, Ed. G., Montreal.
Pozer, C. H., St. George.
Price, D. Edouard, Quebec.
Ryan, Thos., Montreal.
Stevens, G. G., Waterloo.
Trudel, F. X. A., Montreal.
Thibaudeau, Rosaire, Montreal.

PROVINCE OF ONTARIO.

THE HONORABLES

Aikins, J. C., Richview,
Alexander, Geo., Woodstock,
Allan, G. W., Toronto,
Benson, James R., St. Catharines,
Brown, George, Toronto,
Campbell, Alex., Toronto,
Christie, David, Paris,
Dickson, W. H., Niagara,
Flint, Billa, Belleville,
Hamilton, John, Kingston,
Hope, Adam, Hamilton,
Leonard, Elijah, London,
McDonald, Donald, Toronto,
McMaster, W., Toronto,
McPherson, D. L., Toronto,
Read, Robert, Belleville,
Reesor, David, Markham,
Scott, R. W., Ottawa,
Seymour, B., Port Hope,
Shaw, James, Smith's Falls.
Simpson, John, Bowmanville,
Skead, James, Ottawa,
Smith, Frank, Toronto,
Vidal, Alex., Sarnia.

PROVINCE OF NOVA SCOTIA.

THE HONORABLES

Archibald, T. D., Sidney, C. B.,
Bourinot, John, Sidney, C. B.,
Dickey, R. B., Amherst,
Grant, R. P., Pictou,
Kaulback, H. A. N., Lunenburg,

McLelan, A. W., Londonderry,
MacFarlane, A., Wallace,
Miller, W., Arichat,
Northrup, Jeremiah, Halifax,
Power, L. G., Halifax.

PROVINCE OF NEW BRUNSWICK.

THE HONORABLES

Botsford, A. E., Westcork,
Dever, James, St. John,
Fergusson, John, Bathurst,
Glasier, John, Sunbury,
Lewin, J. D., St. John,

McClelan, A. R., Hopewell,
Muirhead, Wm., Chatham,
Odell, W. H., Fredericton,
Wark, David, Richibucto,
Wilmot, R. D., Sunbury.

PROVINCE OF MANITOBA.

THE HONORABLES.

Girard, M. A., St. Boniface, | Sutherland, J., Kildonan.

PROVINCE OF BRITISH COLUMBIA.

THE HONORABLES

Carrall, R. W. W., Victoria,
Cornwall, C. F., Ashcroft,

Macdonald, W. J., Victoria.

PROVINCE OF PRINCE EDWARD ISLAND.

THE HONORABLES

Haythorne, R. P., Charlottetown,
Haviland, T. H., Charlottetown,

Howland, G. W., Alberton,
Montgomery, D., Park Corner.

OFFICIAL DIRECTORY—QUEBEC.

Lieutenant-Governor—The Honorable LUC LETELLIER DE ST. JUST.
Aide-de-Camp and Private Secretary—Capt. F. E. A. GAUTHIER.

EXECUTIVE COUNCIL.

The Honorable H. G. JOLY, Q.C., Premier and Minister of Agriculture and Public Works.
Hon. D. A. ROSS, Attorney-General.
———————————Treasurer.
Hon. F. C. S. LANGELIER, Commissioner of Crown Lands.
Hon. A. CHAUVEAU, Solicitor-General.
Hon. F. G. MARCHAND, Provincial Secretary.
Hon. HENRY STARNES, President of the Council.

LEGISLATIVE COUNCIL.

Hon. Henry Starnes, Speaker.

Hon. Louis Archambault,
" Jean Louis Beaudry,
" George Bryson,
" Chas B. de Boucherville,
" A. R. C. DeLéry,
" P. B. de la Bruère,
" Elizèe Dionne,
" P. E. Dostater,
" James Ferrier,
" Jean E. Gingras,
" Jos. Gaudet,
" John Hearn,

Hon. G. Laviolette,
" F. H. Lemaire,
" Louis Panet,
" J. B. G. Proulx,
" J. E. Prud'homme,
" P. Euclide Roy,
" J. J. Ross,
" Ed. Rèmillard,
" Thos. Savage,
" W. H. Webb,
" Thos. Wood.

G. B. de Boucherville, Secretary.

MEMBERS.

CONSTITUENCIES.	COMMONS.	LOCAL.
Argenteuil............	Dr. Thomas Christie...	Robert J. Meikle..........
Bagot	Joseph A. Mousseau ..	Narcisse Blois.............
Beauce...............	Joseph Bolduc........	Joseph Loirier............
Beauharnois........	Michel Cayley........	Celestin Bergevin.........
Bellechasse.........	A. Larue.............	P. Bontin................
Berthier	Edouard O. Cuthbert..	Joseph Robillard..........
Bonaventure........	Hon. T. Robitaille....	Israel Tarte.............
Brome	E. L. Chandler........	William W. Lynch........
Champlain..........	Hypt. Montplaiser....	Dom. Nap. St. Cyr.......
Chambly............	Pierre B. Benoit	Stanislas Martel, M.D....
Charlevoix	Pierre Tremblay	Onezime Gauthier.........
Châteauguay........	Hon. L. H. Holton....	Edouard Laberge, M.D....
Chicoutimi & Sag'y.	Ernest Cimon.........	William E. Price..........
Compton	Hon. J. H. Pope......	William Sawyer...........
Deux-Montagnes ...	J. B. Daoust	Chas. A. Champagne.....
Dorchester	F. J. Rouleau.........	N. Audet.................
Drummond&Arthab.	D. O. Bourbeau........	William J. Watts.........
Gaspé	Hon. Pierre Fortin....	E. James Flynn ....
Hochelaga..........	Alphonse Desjardins..	Hon. Ls. Beaubien........
Huntingdon	Julius Scriver.........	A. Cameron, M.D.........
Iberville	François Béchard.....	Louis Molleur............
Jacques Cartier.....	Désiré Girouard......	N. M. LeCavalier.........
Joliette.............	Hon. Louis F. G. Baby	Vint. P. Lavallée, M.D....
Kamouraska........	M. Dumont...........	C. A. E. Gagnon..........
Laprairie...........	Alfred Pinsonneault..	L. B. A. Charlebois.......
L'Assomption	Hilaire Hurteau......	Onuphe Peltier...........
Laval..............	Jos. Aldéric Ouimet...	Louis Ons. Loranger......
Levis	Hon. J. G. Blanchet ..	E. T. Paquet, N. P.......
L'Islet.............	Philippe B. Casgrain..	J. B. Dupuis ....
Lotbiniere	Rinfret...............	Hon. Henri G Joly.......
Maskinonge........	Fredéric Houde.......	Edouard Caron ....
Megantic...........	Olivier...............	Hon. G. Irwine...........
Missisquoi.........	G. B. Baker...........	Ernest Racicot...........
Montcalm	Firman Dugas........	Octave Magnon ....
Montmagny	A. C. P. B. Landry...	Louis N. Fortin...........
Montmorency	P. Valin..............	Charles Langelier........
Montreal East......	C. J. Coursol.........	Louis O. Taillon..........
Montreal Centre ...	M. P. Ryan.....	H. A. Nelson ....
Montreal West.....	M. H. Gault..........	James McShane..........
Napierville	Sixte Coupal.........	L. D. Lafontaine, M.D....

DIRECTORY. 209

MEMBERS—Continued.

CONSTITUENCIES.	COMMONS.	LOCAL.
Nicolet	F. X. C. Methot	Chas. Ed. Houde
Ottawa County	Alonzo Wright	Ls. Duhamel, M.D
Pontiac	A. Poupore	L. R. Church, M.D
Portneuf	A. Vallée	Hon. Frs. Langelier
Quebec Centre	J. Malouin	Dr. Rémi F. Rinfret
Quebec West	Thos. McGreevy	A. H. Murphy
Quebec East	Hon. Wilfrid Laurier	Joseph Shehyn
Quebec County	J. P. R. A. Caron	Hon. D. A. Ross
Richelieu	A. Massue	Michel Mathieu
Richmond & Wolfe	Ives	Jacques Picard
Rimouski	Jean B. R. Fiset	Hon. Alex. Chauveau
Rouville	Gigault	Solyme Bertrand
St. Hyacinthe	Louis Tellier	
St. Jean	François Bourassa	Hon. F. G. Marchand
St. Maurice	L.L.L.Desaulniers,MD.	E. S. L. Desaulniers
Shefford	Hon. L. S. Huntington	J. Lafontaine
Sherbrooke	Edward T. Brooks	J. G. Robertson
Soulanges	Jacques P. Lantier	William Duckett
Stanstead	Charles C. Colby	Henry Lovell
Temiscouata	DeGrandbois	George H. Deschêne
Terrebonne	Hon.Louis F.R.Masson	Hon. J. A. Chapleau
Three Rivers	William McDougall	A. Turcotte, Speaker
Vaudreuil	G. B. Mongenais	Emery Lalonde
Vercheres	Hon. Félix Geoffrion	G. B. Brousseau
Yamaska	Charles I. Gill	J. C. S. Wurtele

OFFICIAL DIRECTORY—ONTARIO.

Lieutenant-Governor—The Honorable DONALD ALEXANDER MACDONALD.
Private Secretary—Capt. J. J. FORSYTH.

EXECUTIVE COUNCIL.

Hon. OLIVER MOWAT, Premier and Attorney-General.
" A. S. HARDY, Provincial Secretary.
" AD. CROOKS, Minister of Education.
" C. F. FRASER, Commissioner Public Works.
" T. B. PARDEE, Commissioner of Crown Lands.
" S. C. WOOD, Commissioner of Agriculture and Provincial Treasurer.
Hon. J. G. SCOTT, Secretary.

14

MEMBERS—Continued.

CONSTITUENCIES.	COMMONS	LOCAL.
Addington	J. McRory	Hammel M. Déroche
Algoma		Simon J. Dawson
Brant, South	William Paterson	Hon. Arthur S. Hardy
Brant, North	Gavin Fleming	Hugh Finlayson
Botwell	Hon. David Mills	Hon. A. McKellar
Bruce, North	John Gillies	Donald Sinclair
Bruce, South	A. Shaw	Hon. R. M. Wells, Speaker
Brockville	W. Fitzsimmons	Col. Wilmot H. Cole
Cardwell	Thomas White	John Flesher
Carleton	John Rochester	George W. Monk
Cornwall	Dr. Bergin	John G. Snetsinger
Dufferin	(No representative)	John Barr
Dundas	J. S. Ross	Andrew Broder
Durham, East	Williams	John Rosevear
Durham, West	Herve W. Burk	John McLeod
Elgin, East	T. Arkell	Dr. John H. Wilson
Elgin, West	Geo. E. Casey	Thomas Hodgins
Essex, South	(No representative)	Lewis Wigle
Essex, North	J. C. Patterson	
Frontenac	George A. Kirkpatrick	Delino D. Calvin
Glengarry	John McLennan	Alexander J. Grant
Grenville, South	J. P. Wiser	Hon. Christ. F. Fraser
Grey, North	S. G. Lane	David Creighton
Grey, South	Geo. Jackson	James H. Hunter
Grey, East	D. S. Sproule	Abram. W. Lauden
Haldimand	David Thompson	Jacob Baxter
Halton	W. Macdougall	William D. Lyon
Hamilton	{ Kilvert { Robertson	} James M. Williams.
Hastings, East	John White	Nathaniel S. Appleby
Hastings, West	James Brown	Thos. Wills
Hastings, North	Hon. MacKenz. Bowell	George H. Boulter
Huron, West	Horace Horton	Lt.-Col. Alex. Ross
Huron, South	Malcolm C. Cameron	Archibald Bishop
Huron, North	Thomas Farrow	Thomas Gibson
Kent, West	Rufus Stephenson	A. Coutts
Kent, East	(No representative)	Daniel McCraney
Kingston	Alexander Gunn	William Robinson
Lambton, West	Hon. A. Mackenzie	Hon. T. B. Pardee
Lambton, East	(No representative)	Pierre Graham

DIRECTORY.

MEMBERS—Continued.

CONSTITUENCIES.	COMMONS.	LOCAL.
Lanark, North	Daniel Galbraith	William Mostyn
Lanark, South	John G. Haggart	Abraham Code
Leeds,N.,& Grenville	Charles F. Ferguson	Henry Merrick
Leeds, South	David F. Jones	Robert H. Preston
Lennox	Edmond Hooper	John T. Grange
Lincoln	J. C. Rykert	
London*	John Carling	William R. Meredith
Middlesex, East	Duncan MacMillan	Richard Tooley
Middlesex, North	Timothy Coughlin	John McDougall
Middlesex, West	Geo. W. Ross	John Watterworth
Monck	Lachlin McCallum	Henri R. Haney
Muskoka & Parry Sd.	Alex. P. Cockburn	John C. Miller
Niagara	Patrick Hughes	Hon. S. Richards
Norfolk, North	John Charlton	John F. Clarke
Norfolk, South	William Wallace	Richard Richardson
Northumberland, E.	Joseph Keeler	James M. Ferris
Northumberland, W.	James Cockburn	Wm. Hargraft
Ontario, North	Wheeler	Thomas Paxton
Ontario, South	F. W. Glenn	Nicholas W. Brown
Ottawa City	{ Joseph Tassé { Joseph M. Currier	} D. J. O'Donoghue.
Oxford, North	Thomas Oliver	Hon. Olivier Mowat
Oxford, South	James A. Skinner	Hon. Adam Crooks
Peel	Wm. Elliott	Kenneth Chisholm
Perth, North	Sam. Rollin Hesson	David D. Hay
Perth, South	James Trow	Thomas Ballantyne
Peterborough, East	John Burnham	Dr. John O'Sullivan
Peterborough, West	Geo. Hilliard	William H. Scott
Prescott	Felix Routhier	William Harkin
Prince Edward	Jas. S. McCuaig	Gideon Striker
Renfrew, North	Peter White	Thomas Deacon
Renfrew, South	Wm. Bannerman	James Bonfield
Russell	Hon. John O'Connor	Adam J. Baker
Simcoe, East	(No representative)	John Kean
Simcoe, North	McCarthy	Thomas Long
Simcoe, South	W. C. Little	William MacDougall
Stormont	Oscar Fulton	James Bethune
Toronto, East	Samuel Platt	Hon. M. C. Cameron
Toronto, West	J. R. Robinson	Robert Bell
Toronto, Centre	Robert Hay	(No representative)

DIRECTORY.

Members—Continued.

CONSTITUENCIES.	COMMONS.	LOCAL.
Victoria, North....	Hector Cameron......	Duncan McRae..........
Victoria, South.....	Arthur McQuade......	Hon. S. C. Wood.........
Waterloo, North....	Kranz	Moses Springer..........
Waterloo, South ...	Samuel Merner.......	Isaac Masters ....
Welland	C. W. Bunting........	Hon. J. G. Currie........
Wellington, Centre.	George T. Orton, M.D.	Charles Clarke...........
Wellington, North..	Geo. Alex. Drew.....	John McGowan...........
Wellington, South..	Donald Guthrie......	James Massie............
Wentworth, North..	Thos. Bain...........	James MacMahon........
Wentworth, South..	Jos. Rymal	Wm. Sexton.............
York, North.......	F. W. Strange, M.D...	Dr. J. H. Widdifield......
York, East........	Alfred Boultbee......	John Lane...............
York, West........	Nathaniel Wallace....	Peter Patterson..........

OFFICIAL DIRECTORY—NOVA SCOTIA.

Lieutenant-Governor—The Honorable ADAMS G. ARCHIBALD.
Private Secretary—SAMUEL ADAMS.

EXECUTIVE COUNCIL.

The Honorable S. H. HOLMES, Provincial Secretary and Premier.
" J. S. D. THOMPSON, Attorney-General.
" ——————— Provincial Treasurer.
" SAMUEL CREELMAN, Commissioner Public Works and Mines.
" N. H. WHITE, CHAS. TOWNSEND, ALEX. CAMPBELL, J. S. McDONALD, W. B. TROOP, H. F. McDOUGALL, Ministers without portfolio.

LEGISLATIVE COUNCIL.

Hon. ROBERT BOAK, Jr., President.

Hon. William Armand,
" Slaytey Brown,
" S. Chipman,
" A. McN. Cohran,
" Samuel Creelman,
" W. O. Heffernan,
" Gilbert McKenna,
" J. McKennon,
" Thos. F. Morrison,

Hon. Ed. R. Oakes,
" John Creighton,
" R. Mollison Cutler,
" Chas. Dickie,
" James Fraser,
" D. McN. Parker,
" Peter Smyth,
" Freeman Tupper,
" W. C. Whitman.

DIRECTORY.

MEMBERS.

CONSTITUENCIES.	COMMONS.	LOCAL.
Annapolis	Avard Longley	Hon. W. B. Troop Schafner
Antigonish	Angus McIsaac	John C. McKinnon Whidden
Cape Breton	Wm. McDonald Hugh McLeod	A. J. White E. T. Mosely
Colchester	Thos. McKay	W. A. Patterson Blair
Cumberland	Hon. C. Tupper, C.B.	Ed. Vickery Hon. Chas. Townshead
Digby	John Chipman Wade	John C. Wade Hon. J. S. D. Thompson
Guysborough	Ogden	Joseph W. Hadley A. N. McDonald
Halifax	Malachy B. Daly Mathew H. Richey	Hon. P. C. Hill Hon. J. McDonald W. D. Harrington
Hants	Wm. Henry Allison	Thomas B. Smith Spence
Inverness	Samuel Macdonnell	D. J. Campbell, M.D. Hon. Alex. Campbell
Kings	Fred. W. Borden, M.D.	Fisher Bill
Lunenburg	C. E. Kaulback	J. P. James Smith
Pictou	Hon. Jas. Macdonald Robert Doull	Hon. S. H. Holmes Alex. McKay Bell
Queens	S. T. R. Bill	Bartling Ford
Richmond	Edmond P. Flynn	Leblanc Matheson
Shelbourne	Thos. Robertson	Hon. N. W. White McGray
Victoria	Cameron	David McCurdy Ross
Yarmouth	Frank Killam	Albert Gayton Kinney

OFFICIAL DIRECTORY—NEW BRUNSWICK.

Lieutenant-Governor—The Honorable E. B. CHANDLER.
Private Secretary—Lieutenant-Colonel JOHN SAUNDERS.
Aide-de-Camps—Lieut.-Colonel JOHN SAUNDERS, Captain G. F. KING, and A. F. STREET.

EXECUTIVE COUNCIL.

Hon. ROBERT YOUNG, President.
" GEORGE E. KING, Premier and Attorney-General.
" JOHN J. FRASER, Provincial Secretary.
" B. R. STEVENSON, Inspector-General.
" WILLIAM KELLY, Commissioner of Public Works.
" A. MCQUEEN: J. H. CRAWFORD, EDWARD WILLIS, and W. E. PERLEY without portfolios.

LEGISLATIVE COUNCIL.

.... President

Hon. E. D. Bailey, | Hon. Francis Hibbard,
" John A. Beckwith, | " T. R. Jones,
" Benj. Beveridge, | " John Lewis,
" E. B. Chandler, | " Wm. Lindsay,
" Wm. Hamilton, | " Owen McInervy,
" Daniel Harrington, | " Chas. Perley,
" Archibald Harrison, | " Robert Young.

Alex. McLeod, Secretary.

MEMBERS.

CONSTITUENCIES.	COMMONS.	LOCAL.
Albert	Rogers	Alexander Rogers ...... James Ryan ....
Carleton	Geo. Heber Connell ..	James Leighton .... R. K. Jones ....
Charlotte	Arthur H. Gilmour, jr.	James Murchie .... Hon. B. R. Stevenson .. James McKay .... Thomas Cottrell ....
Gloucester	Hon. T. N. Anglin ...	Kennedy F. Burns ..... Pat. J. Ryan ....
Kent	Guimond	Henry O'Leary .... Urbain Johnson ....

MEMBERS—Continued.

CONSTITUENCIES.	COMMONS.	LOCAL.
King's	James Domville	Hon. J. H. Crawford.... John Flewelling....... Robert E. McLeod.....
Madawaska		Hon. Levi Theriault.....
Northumberland...	Jabez. B. Snowball...	Hon. W. M. Kelly...... William Swim........ Lemuel J. Tweedie.... Allan A. Davidson.....
Queen's	King	Walter S. Butler...... Francis Woods........
Restigouche	George Haddow	Archib. McKenzie..... John Phillips........
St. John, City	Hon. Sam. L. Tilley..	Hon W Wedderburn,Spkr Rob. Marshall.........
St. John, County...	Isaac Burpee...... Chas. W. Weldon..	Henry A. Austin....... Hon. C. E. King....... Hon. Ed. Willis....... William Elder........
Sunbury	Charles Burpee	Hon. W. E. Perley..... Hon. John S. Covert...
Victoria	J. Costigan	William B. Beveridge....
Westmorland	Hon. A. J. Smith	Ed. J. Smith.......... A. McQueen .... John A. Humphrey.... Thomas Rickard.......
York	John Pickard	Hon. John J. Fraser...; Thomas T. Barker..... Robert Robinson...... Hiram Dow, M. D......

OFFICIAL DIRECTORY—PRINCE EDWARD ISLAND.

Lieutenant-Governor—The Honorable Sir ROBERT HODGSON.
Aides-de-Camp—Lieut.-Colonel JOHN LONGWORTH, R. R. HODGSON.

HOUSE OF COMMONS.

S. F. PERRY and JAMES YEO, Prince County.
Hon. J. C. POPE and FRED DE ST. C. BRECKEN, Queen's County.
Hon. DANIEL DAVIS and DR. MCINTYRE, County of King.

DIRECTORY.

EXECUTIVE COUNCIL.

Hon. L. H. DAVIS, Premier and Attorney-General.
" G. W. DEBLOIS, Provincial Secretary.
" W. D. STEWART, Public Works.
" G. GORDON, S. PROWSE, J. F. ROBERTSON, J. LEFURGY, JOHN YEO, and A. LAIRD, members of the Council without portfolios.

LEGISLATIVE COUNCIL.

Honorable John Balderston, President.

Hon. Simon Bolger,
" Thomas W. Dodd,
" Daniel McDonald,
" Wm. McGill,
" R. Munn,

Hon. Alex. Laird,
" R. B. Reid,
" W. G. Strong,
" Jos. Wightman,
" A. McEwen.

LEGISLATIVE ASSEMBLY.

Hon. Corneilus Howatt, Speaker.

Prince, 1st District, Nich. Conroy, Edward Hackett.
Prince, 2d " Hon. John Yeo, J. W. Richards.
Prince, 3rd " Hon. J. O. Arsenault, John A. Macdonald.
Prince, 4th " John R. Calhoun, W. C. Lea.
Prince, 5th " Hon. John Lefurgey, Angus MacMillan.
Georgetown, Hon. Daniel Gordon, L. J. Westaway.
Kings, 1st District, Lauchlin Macdonald, James R. McLean.
Kings, 2nd " Hon. W. W. Sullivan, Hilary McIsaac.
Kings, 3rd " John G. Scrimgeour, J. E. McDonald.r
Kings, 4th " James Robertson, Sam. Prowse.
Charlottetown, Hon. Louis H. Davis, Geo. W. DeBlois.
Queen, 1st District, Wm. Campbell, W. D. Stewart.
Queen, 2nd " Donald McKay, Donald Farquharson.
Queen, 3rd " Hon. Frs. Kelly, Henry Beer.
Queen, 4th " John F. Robertson, Wm. Welsh.

OFFICIAL DIRECTORY—BRITISH COLUMBIA.

Lieutenant-Governor—The Honorable ALBERT MARTIN RICHARDS.
Private Secretary—GEORGE R. LAYTON.

EXECUTIVE COUNCIL.

Hon. ANDREW C. ELLIOTT, Premier and Attorney-General.
" FORBES G. VERNON, Commissioner Public Works.
" WM. SMITH, Minister of Finance and Agriculture.

MEMBERS OF THE COMMONS.

J. SPENCER THOMPSON, Cariboo.
JAMES CUNNINGHAM, New Westminster.
ARTHUR BUNSTER, Vancouver.
ARMAND DE COSMOS and CAPTAIN ROSCOE, Victoria.
EDWARD DEWDNEY, Yale.

LEGISLATIVE ASSEMBLY.

Hon. James Trimble, Speaker.

Hon. George A. Walkem, Geo. Cowan, John Evans, Cariboo.
John Ash, M. D., Comox.
Hon. Wm. Smith, E. Pimbury, Cowichan.
Wm. Fisher, F. Williams, Esquimault.
R. L. E. Gilbraith, Chas. Gallagher, Kootenay.
Wm. Brown, Wm. Morrison, Lillooet.
John Bryden, Nanaimo.
Robert Dickinson, New Westminster.
Ebenezer Brown, Hon. W. J. Armstrong, New Westminster.
Hon. T. B. Humphreys, Dr. Tolmie, Victoria
Hon. James Trimble, Hon. O. C. Elliott, J. W. Douglas, Hon. Robert Beanen, Victoria.
Hon. F. G. Vernon, J. A. Mara, Robt. Smith, Yale.

OFFICIAL DIRECTORY—MANITOBA.

Lieutenant-Governor—The Honorable JOSEPH EDWARD CAUCHON.

EXECUTIVE COUNCIL.

Hon. JOHN NORQUAY, Premier and Treasurer.
" D. M. WALKER, Attorney-General.
" JOSEPH ROYAL, Minister of Public Works.
" C. P. BROWN, Provincial Secretary.

LOCAL HOUSE.

Hon. Jos. Dubuc, Speaker.

F. Chenier, Baie St. Paul.	Hon. M. A. Girard, St. Boniface.
John Taylor, Headingly.	A. Murray, St. Charles.
Dr. Cowan, High Bluff.	Thos. Howard, St. Clement.
J. Sutherland, Kildoman.	Max. Lepine, St. Frs.-Xavier, East.
Hon. J. McKay, Loc Manitoba.	Hon. Jos. Royal, do. West.
F. E. Cornish, Pte-aux-Peupliers.	E. Bourque, St. Jacques.
K. McKenzie, Portage La Prairies.	Hon. Jos. Dubuc, St. Norbert.
W. F. Lucton, Rockwood.	M. Black, St. Paul.
A. F. Martin, Ste. Agathe.	Jos. Lemay, St. Vital.
Chas. Nolin, Ste. Anne.	W. R. Dick, Springfield.
John Gunn, St. André North.	C. P. Brown, Westbourne.
Hon. J. Norquay, St. André South.	R. A. Davis, Winnipeg.

MEMBERS OF HOUSE OF COMMONS.

Hon. DONALD A. SMITH, Selkirk.
JOSEPH DUBUC, Provencher.
JOHN CHRISTIN SCHULTZ, Lisgar.
Sir JOHN A. MACDONALD, Marquette.

OFFICIAL DIRECTORY—NORTH-WEST.

Lieutenant-Governor—The Honorable DAVID MILLS.

EXECUTIVE COUNCIL.

MATHEW RYAN and HUGH RICHARDSON, Stipendiary Magistrates.
Lieut.-Colonel J. F. MCLEOD, C.M.G., Commissioner of Police.
A. E. FORGET, Secretary.
WM. J. SCOTT, Registrar.
Lieut.-Colonel A. G. IRVINE, Assistant-Commissioner of Police.
M. ST. JOHN, Sheriff.
M. G. DICKINSON, Indian Agent.

www.ingramcontent.com/pod-product-compliance
Lightning Source LLC
Chambersburg PA
CBHW031627160426
43196CB00006B/309